INNOVATION

Turning ON Innovation in Your
Culture, Teams, and Organization

TERRY JONES

FOUNDER OF TRAVELOCITY AND FOUNDING CHAIRMAN OF KAYAK.COM

This book is dedicated to Max Hopper and Bob Crandall of American Airlines. Leaders, mentors, and innovators, they set me on my creative journey.

ON Innovation

Table of Contents

INTRODUCTION

"The credit belongs to the man who is actually in the arena, whose face is marred by dust and sweat and blood, who strives valiantly, who errs and comes up short again and again...and who, at the best, knows, in the end, the triumph of high achievement, and who, at the worst, if he fails, at least he fails while daring greatly, so that his place shall never be with those cold and timid souls who knew neither victory nor defeat."
—*Theodore Roosevelt*

If innovation isn't happening in your company, it might be trapped below the Bozone Layer.

That's the impenetrable layer of middle management that often stops good ideas from moving up the chain of command.

The ideas are there. Good ones, I'll bet. They're just trapped.

It isn't middle management's fault. It's the culture.

As companies grow, they become risk averse. They focus on optimizing errorless production at high speed.

Errors are ruthlessly eliminated. Failure is not an option.

Managers know there is no percentage in taking risk, so they don't.

Yet, innovation requires experimentation and failure.

I'm speaking from experience.

I've worked in ten start-ups in my career. In each, we spent much of our time experimenting, failing, adapting, and experimenting again until a new, workable outcome was created that went to market.

Working in those companies, I've learned that innovation rests on the twin pillars of a culture that fosters innovation and a team that can successfully deliver that innovation to market.

This book is filled with seventy-two ideas on how to do that. I hope, as Steve Jobs put it, it helps you put a "dent in the universe."

HOW TO READ THIS BOOK

I hope you find this book instantly useful.

You won't find long, dense chapters of scientific research and ivory-tower theories.

Instead, you will find short, pithy chapters with real-world insights and actions that can help you and your company be successful innovators.

I know you're busy, so I've designed the book so you can pick it up, read for ten minutes, and take away an action nugget you can use today.

Although the *sections* are arranged in the progressive order of the innovation process, it isn't necessary to read the *chapters* in order.

Feel free to read from front to back, back to front, or just drop in wherever you wish.

Although I chose to discuss creating a team before creating a culture, there is no right order. You must know what culture you want to create in order to build the right team. The team you select will also create the culture. You must think about both at once.

Research shows we are more likely to act on what we learn if we imprint it with several senses.

So as you *read* this book, *write* down how you plan to follow up, and *discuss* possible applications with your colleagues; you're much more likely to turn your insights into real-world results.

Try to answer the questions at the end of each chapter. They not only serve as a summary of the main idea of the chapter, but they can also be used at staff meetings to catalyze discussions about the role and process of innovation in your company.

When you finish this book, don't put it away on a shelf. Keep it handy on your desk.

Whenever you encounter a stalemate, open it up to a random page. The idea in that chapter may be just the fresh perspective you need to approach that situation differently and move it forward.

Ready? Turn the page, and let's innovate.

FOREWORD

What Is Innovation Anyway?

*"Creativity is about **thinking** up new things.*
*Innovation is about **doing** new things."*
—*Theodore Levitt*

While there are many definitions of innovation, this is the one I like the best.

I am the holder of four patents of what I think are great ideas.

Unfortunately, that is all they are. *Ideas.* They have never been turned into products. They are not, at least not yet, innovations.

While this book discusses various processes for creating ideas, its primary focus is on building cultures, teams, and prototypes, creating business models, testing and changing ideas, and putting them to work.

My brother, Dewitt Jones, a *National Geographic* photographer for many years, is wonderfully creative. He's retired now from the *Geographic*, but still delivers keynotes on how to "Make Your Life Your Art" to top organizations around the world.

One of his pursuits these days is "iPhoneography." He uses his iPhone to create exquisite photos he shares on Facebook.

That's creativity, and it's great fun. But it's when he charges (and gets) a fee for people to come to his iPhoneography seminars on "How to Create and Sell Your Photos" that his creativity turns into innovation.

When the Internet bubble burst in 2000, hundreds of Internet companies failed. More than one hundred thousand people were thrown out of work.

Why did so many of these companies fail? I believe it was because many of them were little more than a PowerPoint deck that had raised money!

The start-up team had an idea, sometimes a good idea, and they were able to raise lots of money for that idea. They hired a bunch of friends (sometimes talented ones) and threw a great launch party, but then they had no step-by-step process for moving forward.

Many I met had no practical experience with budgets or business models. They didn't understand how to create the culture they needed or the team that was required. In short, they didn't understand how to turn their idea into real-world innovation.

At Travelocity, we were lucky. Many of us were American Airlines veterans. We'd been through American's proven process of delivering quality products to thousands of people every day, week after week, month after month.

Combining that expertise with a focused team, lots of money, and, at the same time, shedding the bureaucracy of the big company was the secret sauce to successfully putting our idea to work.

As you read this book, keep in mind that your goal is to put your ideas to *work*. Creating the culture, selecting the team, soliciting and then selecting viable ideas...all are just steps along the way to producing bottom-line value in the marketplace.

SECTION 1:

What's the Rush?
What Are the Business Changes
Demanding Innovation Today?

"It does not do to leave a dragon out of your plans if you live near him."

—*J. R. R. Tolkien,* The Hobbit

"Never, ever, think outside the box."

What's Your Organization's Attitude
toward Change?

*"One of the things that is mind-boggling right now
is how much we have to change all the time."*
—Anne Mulcahy, former CEO, Xerox[1]

I've made presentations on innovation to more than forty thousand people over the past few years. I enjoy talking with anyone who wants to continue the conversation following my speech.

While the questions vary by industry, the urgency these people feel is usually the same. They see the world changing around them and realize they have to change to keep up with it.

Unfortunately, while *they* understand the need to change, it often seems their bosses or coworkers don't.

In fact, one attendee said, "My CEO attended this event with me. I'm glad we heard your speech together, because it's going to pave the way for me to broach the subject (again) of how urgent it is for us to do more to increase innovation in our company."

Are you in a position where you need to convince others to be more supportive of innovation?

If so, this section outlines many important changes affecting business today and makes a case for why it's in the best interests of organizations to innovate with these changes in mind...*now.*

Hopefully, reflecting on how these changes affect your business will spark your idea engine. You might want to reference these changes to convince your boss and team of the urgent need to more actively encourage innovation in your organization.

Questions to Kick-Start Innovation

1. On a scale of 1 to 10 (1 = nonexistent and 10 = excellent), how does your organization rank in its support of innovation? Explain your ranking.
2. What's a tangible example of how your organization has encouraged and advanced innovation?
3. Do you feel a sense of urgency about this issue? Is your organization not adapting quickly enough to changes in your industry? What's an example?

Short-Circuited or Rewired Distribution

"The only danger is not to evolve."
—*Jeff Bezos, Amazon.com*

I began my career as a travel agent in 1970. In those days, customers called us with their flight needs, and we called the airline to book their trips. More than 90 percent of all airline tickets were sold that way.

That began to change (and change quickly) when we introduced Travelocity in 1996. Our innovation created a short circuit in the distribution system of how flights were bought and sold.

As online travel agencies continued to evolve, they captured $50 billion of the air travel business.

In addition, airlines then got into the act and started recruiting travelers to come directly to their websites to book flights with their preferred carrier. Next, the airlines cut travel agent ticket commissions to zero (that's right, zero), dooming most leisure agents.

In ten short years, more than eighteen thousand travel agents were out of business.

Similar innovations have happened in the music business.

I used to go to Tower Records (remember them?) and buy the latest CD of my favorite group.

Once Apple invented iTunes and the iPod, millions of music lovers, including me, flocked to the new intermediary, Apple. Over a very short period, CD sales plummeted, and traditional music companies lost 35 percent of their value.[2]

Brick and mortar bookstores (i.e., Borders) have also been short- circuited by a combination of new technology, a disruption of their traditional distribution, and new intermediaries.

Yet not all businesses are being short-circuited. Some are being what I call "rewired."

The air-conditioning industry is an example of that. In a keynote to the Air Conditioning Manufacturing and Dealers Association, I marveled at how much things have changed since I bought an air conditioner for my Dallas home in the '90s.

Back then I looked in the Yellow Pages to find a local dealer. A display ad for Johnson's caught my eye. My friends had good things to say about them, so I drove to a local store that weekend. A salesman asked about my needs, showed me a wide selection of options, and then suggested a Trane. I trusted his advice and experience, so I bought one on the spot.

How would I buy an air conditioner today? I'd open my laptop and check out the manufacturer websites, some review sites, and perhaps a price comparison site. I'd make a decision and contact the manufacturer directly, who would refer my lead to a local dealer, who would then call me to close the deal and make an appointment to deliver and install my unit.

It is a new, rewired relationship. If your company name includes the word "agent" or "broker," or if you have a multilayered distribution system, chances are, you are being rewired.

This trend doesn't exclude anyone. You can't hide just because you sell only B2B. Those relationships are being rewired as well.

And don't give me that line, "Our products are sold, not bought."

If your salesperson makes a wonderful sales call, what's the first thing I will do when he leaves? I'll open my laptop and find your competitor. And by the way, if you are the competitor and aren't online, then I'll never find you.

Stores are turning into showrooms. Just walk into the electronics department of a Best Buy, Costco, or your favorite department store. Most people have their cell phones out and are checking around to make sure they're getting the best deal possible on their flat screen, stereo, or computer.

Want good news? It is possible (and preferable) for *you* to rewire your business rather than have it rewired for you.

You don't have to be short-circuited out of existence, like the thousands of travel agents who could not adapt. It's in your best interests to take a proactive, rather than passive, role, so innovation is being done *by* you instead of *to* you.

Questions to Kick-Start Innovation

1. Has your industry been short-circuited by an innovation in the distribution process? Explain.
2. Or are you in a business that has been rewired? How so?
3. What's an example of how your company has taken a proactive vs. passive role in adapting to changes?

Search

"You cannot step twice into the same stream."
—*Plato*

Unless you can say with confidence about your company, "We've got something you can't Google," you'd better pay attention to search.

Almost *half* of Google's daily searches are for products or services. On top of that, search is predicted to influence *more than half* of US retail sales by 2014.[3]

We know the power of search well at Kayak.com.

We are not only a search company ourselves (vertical travel search), but we got almost *all* our customers through search in the first five years of our existence. It was a *very* successful strategy, with measurable results, and it cost substantially less than we would have spent on brand advertising.

Yet search can be a big problem for traditional companies. As customers search for products, the search can quickly devolve to a price-only focus.

On the other hand, search might be the *only* way people will ever find your company or product. With more than fifteen thousand new products being introduced every year in the grocery category alone, how can you stand out?[4]

SC Johnson, the makers of OFF!, bought the URL Mosquitoes.com for this very reason.

People irritated by mosquito bites search the web for solutions, and this site pops up first. People want to be rid of mosquitoes, and this site tells them that OFF! is the answer to their problem.

A friend of mine was in a hurry and threw all his dirty laundry in the washer. Unfortunately, a red shirt dyed his white underwear pink. He tried to bleach them back to white, but it didn't work. So he went to the grocery store and asked, "Do you have something to remove this type of stain?"

"Nope," came the reply.

So he drove home (this was before he could have used a smartphone) and searched online for an answer. The University of Iowa website (go figure) revealed that RIT, the dye company, also sold stain remover.

Back to the store my friend went. He asked a stock clerk, "Do you have RIT dye remover?"

"Nope," was the answer again.

Undaunted, he searched and found RIT stain remover hiding on the bottom shelf.

The moral of this story? You can no longer expect store clerks to know your product exists, much less whether they stock it. You are no longer competing at the *brand* level; you are competing at the *search* level...the individual product level.

Even if you do have something that can't be Googled (whether that's a unique product, service, or pricing model that is yours alone), then how will your story get heard and seen by your target customers?

In the twenty-first century, in addition to shelf space, you have to have "search space."

Focus not on the fact that people are not necessarily using search to find your product, but on what it does. At REI (the outdoor equipment store) you can search for "ice climbing," which of course they don't sell. They gather products together in virtual groups to connect buyers with their passions.

Even if you're local rather than national, this still applies to you. Did you know more than 20 percent of Google searches are for *local* business?

You have to be in Google Local, and your listing must link to your brick and mortar location *and* your online site...or you will be ignored because people don't know you exist.

Bottom line? The secret of search is being *found*.

Questions to Kick-Start Innovation

1. Are you prepared for the changes search is bringing to your business? Are you leveraging them? How so?
2. What's your Mosquitoes.com? What words do people use to search problems your products solve? What words do they look for that are associated with your topic, services, or issue?
3. Have you claimed and developed those domains so you're harvesting the rewards of those searches?

IDEA 4

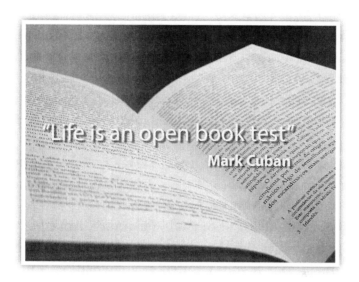

"Life is an open book test"
Mark Cuban

Information Has Escaped!

*"Your customers will know more about your business than you do in
a very short time. You have twenty-four to thirty-six months to get ready."*
—Ken Chenault, CEO, American Express

We've all done it. Someone poses a question, and we quickly become the brightest person in the room by whipping out our smartphone and reciting the right answer…in seconds.

Anything we want or need to know is available free, at the click of a button. This is changing the way business works.

In the past, we had to go to an "agent" (i.e., a travel, real estate, or insurance agent) to get industry "insider" information. It was impossible to access agents' special information, which gave them the power to act as middlemen. It was their secret sauce.

No more. Businesses based on information scarcity are rapidly becoming irrelevant...unless they adapt.

I was preparing a speech for a major insurance company. I asked the president, "What key message would you like me to focus on with your agents?"

He thought about it for a moment and said, "Tell them, in a nice way, if they think they'll be selling auto insurance in five years, they're nuts!"

That's because the information customers need to compare a company's features and prices is available online, all the time.

Plus, some smart companies are making it *really* easy to apply online for insurance. For example, GEICO allows you to use an app where you take a photo of your driver's license, e-mail it with a few more details, and voila, you are done!

We're not just talking about auto insurance. Amazingly, 40 percent of life insurance purchases are not made face to face.[5]

The conclusion? If your company's information is not online, your customer will go somewhere else. It's no longer possible to try to create value through information scarcity.

You can use information to customize the *advice* you give customers, but assume they've already read what you were planning to present to them. Review their specific needs and interests, then move to providing personalized recommendations.

Remember, you are no longer the sole source of information about your products. Between tweets, Facebook, blog posts, Yelp, and other online reviews, there is as much, if not more, information about your product online from others as from you!

When I moved into a new house, I couldn't get my remote to turn on the Sony audio receiver. I read the manuals and called the Sony support desk. They were no help.

After two years of frustration, I decided to try again. This time, I found the answer to my problem on an obscure message board (you had to press three unconnected buttons at once). Why didn't Sony know that?

Dell solves this problem by searching the web for all mentions of their product and creating "certified answers." By monitoring customer needs and providing answers to frequently asked questions, they augment and improve the information and experience associated with their products.

Questions to Kick-Start Innovation

1. Does your industry employ "agents"? How has your company adapted to the fact that information about your products, services, and prices is available anytime, anywhere?
2. If you are a manufacturer, do you realize that *you* have to provide as much information to the consumer as your dealer?
3. How are you, like Dell, monitoring customer needs and questions and being proactive in providing that information?

The Death of Distance

"Location, location, location."
—*William Dillard, founder, Dillard's Department Store*

Location has been the mantra for retail since the first Neolithic trade fair, but that is certainly changing now.

Travelocity was the largest travel agency in Fargo, North Dakota. Of course, we weren't located in Fargo, we were in cyberspace!

While CEO at Travelocity, I received this e-mail from a customer. "My name is Nina. I am a farm wife. Each year I try and do something new. Last year I rode a taxi for the first time while in Denver. This year I booked our vacation on Travelocity.com!"

Intrigued, I called Nina, but got a recording saying, "Sorry I'm not here right now; it's town day." When I did reach Nina, she told me it was so far to town that it took an entire day to go there, shop, and return. That was a new idea for this city boy!

She told me Travelocity had totally changed the way she booked travel. She now spends as much time as she wants shopping from home and doesn't need to "waste" a town day on that.

Location (at least physical location) is still important in retail, but without an online location as well, your business may not make it.

Even if you convince the customer to come to your convenient location, your competitor is only a click away. You no longer have to drive across town to get a better price. Did you know 38 percent of smartphone users have stopped a purchase because they found a better price in another store *while in your store*?[6]

The death of distance isn't all downside. The upside is you can now sell worldwide, regardless of where you are. The entire world is now both your marketplace and your competitor.

My brother lives on the remote island of Molokai. When a forest fire burned near his home, it took way too long for the fire department to arrive. His home was saved, but he decided to be proactive in case it happened again.

He called the biggest hardware store in the islands to buy some fire hose. "Well," the vendor said, "I can order some for you, but it's very expensive because it has to come from the mainland."

The price was triple what he expected to pay, so he got creative. He went online and discovered a website that sold used fire hoses. Turns out regulations mandate that fire brigades change their hoses (worn out or not) every few years. Dewitt bought a used hose, shipped from the East Coast, for a fraction of what he would have paid for a new one from Oahu, sixty miles away.

Questions to Kick-Start Innovation

1. How is your organization dealing with the death of distance?
2. How are you making distance work *for* vs. *against* you?

Big Data

"Experts sometimes possess more data than judgment."
—*Colin Powell*

When I was running the American Airlines reservations system (known as SABRE) in the early '90s, we were proud that we had a *terabyte* of data. A terabyte of data was an unusually large amount at that time. It cost more than $10 million and took up thousands of square feet.

Now a terabyte costs $75 and can fit in the palm of your hand. The drop in the price of storage has been matched by the increase in data collection. According to IBM, 90 percent of the world's data has been created in just the past *two years.*[7]

Unfortunately, big data doesn't always mean big wisdom! As Powell pointed out, people who possess data must use judgment to leverage it to its full potential.

At Travelocity, we saved every ticket customers bought *and* every search they ever made. This allowed us to laser-target customers based on their expressed intentions and buying history.

The chief technology officer at Walmart (which has an immense database) told me they found a public database that geo-located the largest concentrations of private swimming pools in the United States. Then they cross-referenced that with their store locations. *Overnight* they became the largest seller of pool chemicals in the United States.

I'm an advisor to a company called Sojern, which produces advertising on your airline boarding passes. Because they receive all your airline website search information, as soon as you finished searching for flights to San Diego for your family of four, they begin offering you San Diego hotels. As soon as you make a reservation for your hotel, a car rental ad and entertainment options in the area pop up. These ads follow you all over the web. Each interaction creates more data, which creates more specifically targeted ads.

Does your organization collect and leverage big data? If you don't, your competitor probably does. If they create "big wisdom" before you...well, you know the rest of that story.

Questions to Kick-Start Innovation

1. How is your company collecting and leveraging big data?
2. What is one specific example of how you're using it to get better profiles of customer preferences and purchases?
3. How are you giving your company a competitive edge by doing something innovative with big data that others in your industry aren't?

Business Model Evolution

*"Anything you're rigid about, sooner or later, the rug is
going to get pulled out from under you."*
—Alan Arkin, American actor

I grew up in a small town with one bookstore, one record store, and one movie theater. We used the newspaper classifieds, Yellow Pages, and the encyclopedia (remember those?) to find out what we needed to know.

Then the mall moved in at the edge of town. All our small businesses were changed forever.

In came Barnes & Noble, Best Buy, and a megaplex movie theater. All of a sudden, competing "yellow page" books cropped up. Encarta came out on CD.

Next came the Internet. And with it Amazon, "the world's largest bookstore," and CDNow, "the most CDs."

First Blockbuster, then Netflix started cutting into movie theater revenue with their rent-a-video-and-watch-it-at-home options.

Then eBay went after newspaper classifieds (which are the primary source of newspaper revenue). Big Yellow brought the Yellow Pages online, and Encarta went online as well.

Then those "new" business models evolved.

Amazon came out with the Kindle and now sells more digital books than physical books.

The iPod made CDs virtually obsolete.

Streaming video ushered in YouTube and Hulu. Blockbuster stores were soon empty, then shut down.

Craigslist and Angie's List offered do-it-yourself online classifieds, for free, drastically reducing the lifeblood revenue of the industry.

Crowdsourced Wikipedia put the printed encyclopedia (and God knows how many encyclopedia salesmen) out of business.

We're witnessing yet more evolution as the mobile, social, and local movements are changing business models yet again. Pandora offers streaming music; Spotify does it in a social context. Apps let you read e-books on many devices. Google Maps are better than yellow pages.

Study the Evolutionary Business Grid below, and the second one about mobile and social. Add a row for your organization and industry on this table.

Make this the topic of your next staff meeting. Ask employees to ponder how quickly your model could be affected by newly emerging technologies. Ask for their input as to how you can get ahead of this curve instead of being crushed by it.

Traditional	Selection & Price	On–Line	Speed & Convenience
Bookstore	Barnes & Noble	Amazon	Kindle
Record Store	Best Buy	CD Now	Itunes
Movie Theatre	Megaplex Theatre	Netflix	YouTube
Newspaper Classifieds		eBay	craigslist
Yellow Pages	Competing Books	Big Yellow	Angie's List
Encyclopedia	Encarta	Encarta On–Line	Wikipedia

Traditional	Mobile/Social
Bookstore	Reader App
Record Store	Pandora/Spotify
Movie Theatre	Hulu/Socialcam
Newspaper Classifieds	Facebook
Yellow Pages	Yelp
Encyclopedia	Google

Questions to Kick-Start Innovation

1. What mobile, social, and local "revolutions" are affecting your industry and company? How so?
2. Perhaps it isn't your product that needs changing. Could the issue be how you bring it to market?
3. How can your organization be the change agent rather than be short-circuited by emerging technologies?

IDEA 8

More Forces Driving Change

*"Consumers are transforming faster than we are, and
if we don't catch up, we're in trouble."*
—Ian Schafer, CEO, Deep Focus

There are many forces of change impacting the way people do business that may influence the way you operate.

Spend thirty minutes online studying the *Wall Street Journal*'s annual Technology Innovation Awards: http://tinyurl.com/99cwke9.

I make it a point to check them out every year because it's like reading the writing on the wall for innovation.

It's easy to get insular. We become specialists in our own indus-try and then get blindsided by influences from other fields we weren't even aware of or weren't paying attention to.

The categories in the innovation awards are worth consider-ing. Or just scan the headlines of popular magazines, and you'll see articles on 3-D printing, solar shingles, handheld sonograms, mobile payments, and dozens of other developments that might change your business.

Another trend is that *convenience trumps quality*. People would rather have "good enough" *right now* than wait for "better" *later.*

As actress Carrie Fisher says, "Instant gratification takes too long." Speed is more attractive than excellence. For example:

- MP3 sound quality isn't as good as records.
- Camera phones aren't as good as Nikons.
- Mobile games aren't as good as console games.

In some cases the convenient option is even better than the traditional one. Many think that online newspapers, because they are interactive and instant, are better than the ink-on-paper ver-sions. A lifelong book reader, I prefer the Kindle to paper books because Kindle books are instantly available, don't fill up my briefcase, and there are no pages to blow around while reading on the beach!

The convenience over quality movement has eaten whole industries. What will eat yours if you don't innovate?

Questions to Kick-Start Innovation

1. Have you studied a list of this year's innovation award winners? What trends did you see that affect you?
2. What is one way you are proactively adapting to influences and develop-ments from other industries?

SECTION 2:

Create a Team that Facilitates Innovation

"As we look ahead into the next century, leaders will be those who empower others."
—*Bill Gates*

Who Should Lead Your Innovation Effort?

"The key to successful leadership today is influence, not authority."
—Kenneth Blanchard

It was luck that I was the right leader, at the right time, for Travelocity. Because I had been a travel agent, I was assigned to shepherd our online travel efforts. But if someone had done a CEO search, I happened to have the right combination of experience and expertise for the job.

- I started my working life as a travel agent.
- I spent ten years leading software product design groups.

- I spent five years leading software development of large products on a worldwide basis.
- I spent four years running one of the largest computer systems and networks in the world.
- I'd worked in two start-ups and was a vice president in a multibillion-dollar corporation.

I didn't know it at the time, but this experience contributed to what was basically a PhD in how to run and grow the first large-scale online travel agency.

I've thought a lot about the qualities needed to lead innovative efforts. It can be hard to find all these qualities in one person, but it's worth using this as a checklist when searching for a leader who has what it takes to create a team that rewards innovation.

1. **Networked.** No team will have *all* the resources it needs to complete its task and achieve its goals. They will have to get help from other departments or companies. A leader with strong networking skills is essential to create the collaborations that will be needed.
2. **Coaching.** Coaches *shape* performance—they don't *shame* it. They don't just send players to the minors when they make a mistake. They help team members evaluate mistakes, make necessary adjustments, and integrate lessons learned so they perform better…next time.
3. **Inspiring**. The leader has to be able to motivate team members to reach group goals, not because they *have* to, but because they *want* to. Boring mission statements won't work. The leader needs to be a visionary who can create excitement about the future.
4. **Broad Minded.** Leaders need to stay open to new ideas and processes. As discussed in Idea 19, the words "but we've always done it this way" shall never be uttered.

5. **Fearless.** Generally impervious to criticism. They listen for merit but don't take it personally and don't let naysayers divert the team from moving ahead.
6. **Powerful.** The leader has to have "clout in the house." He or she needs to be high enough in the organization hierarchy to get initiatives approved and funded.

Questions to Kick-Start Innovation

1. Are you hiring a leader for your innovation team? Review the qualities on this list. How do your lead candidates score? Which are their strongest/weakest qualities?

IDEA 10

How Should You Organize for Innovation?

"For me, my role is about unleashing what people already have inside them that is suppressed in most work environments."
—*Tony Hsieh, founder and CEO of Zappos*

Can an innovation committee work?

As I discuss in section 6, "Increase Innovation in a Large Corporation," it can be tough to run successful innovation committees in a big-company environment.

If you are creating cross-functional committees representing many divisions (the operative word), it can be challenging to win buy-in and gain loyalty to radically new ideas.

But committees *can* work when they focus on a *single* problem or process.

The president of a medium-sized business told me she'd recently formed an innovation committee and asked for volunteers. Not surprisingly, almost all her volunteers were young people.

These millennials immediately started leveraging the lens of their everyday experience to update standard operating procedures.

They asked permission to turn the company newsletter into a blog. (Duh.) Their twentysomething age and ubiquitous use of social media and mobile technology created a common bond.

Common bonds are very important for committee success because they fast-forward trust and a feeling of mutuality.

What about an innovation laboratory? Idea 42, called "What Happened to the Lab?" explains the pros and cons of this option. For now, I'd suggest you skip the lab process unless you are a very large company that needs basic scientific research. Today your business *is* the lab.

If your new idea is a radical departure from what you do today, you might consider a separate organization, removed from the corporate structure. Free it from the bureaucracy that all large organizations have so it can fly. There is more on this section 6.

However you organize, the leader must give "air cover" and make a visible commitment to sponsor and guide innovation efforts. Without the strong voice of a top leader making it clear that innovation will be supported, it doesn't stand a chance.

Even with that commitment, innovation is more like running an obstacle course than a sprint. There are always minefields along the way.

A woman came up to me after one of my presentations and said, "What do you do when an idea is stuck?"

When I asked her to explain, she said, "We had a great idea, presented it to the president, and he approved it to move forward. Now, middle managers from different departments are trying to kill it."

I said, "It's good you got the president involved in the beginning. Now you need to use his influence to keep the idea alive."

I told her to give him a weekly report on each idea he has approved. Indicate the status on each: *red* (stopped in its tracks), *yellow* (in limbo or slower-than-expected progress), and *green* (moving forward efficiently and effectively). Give the reasons for yellow and red status. If middle managers know the president is getting those reports which detail their stall tactics, they will come around quickly.

In another way to handle this, many corporations have highly trained innovation "mentors" or Six Sigma "black belts" who can be assigned to help existing teams function optimally.

How you organize for innovation depends on a lot of factors, ranging from how disruptive the idea is to how experienced your team is. Instead of there being one recommended formula, take into account the different factors mentioned in this chapter.

Questions to Kick-Start Innovation

1. Do you have an innovation committee in your organization? Do the members have a single goal or purpose? If not, "How's that workin' for ya?"
2. Do your innovation committee members have a common bond (like the tech-savvy millennials)? What is it?
3. Do you have a leader who is a vocal supporter of innovation? How does he or she give "air cover" and gain support for innovative ideas and initiatives?

How Do You Select Members
of Your Innovation Team?

"When all think alike, then no one is thinking."
—*Walter Lippman*

It's as important to select the right team members as it is to pick the right idea.

Don't automatically accept whoever the HR department recommends or other departments foist upon you. Insist, or strongly request, on the autonomy to personally select members so you have all-important diversity.

Bring in longtime employees and people who are just starting out. Find what the famous Apple commercial called "the misfits, the rebels, the ones who think differently."[8]

Our initial Travelocity team was like that. They were self-described rebels who had self-selected to work on a risky project.

As Travelocity grew, I fought very hard to hire from outside our parent company. I wanted to find people who were actively involved in the Internet and people *without* travel experience to debate the travel experts we already had on our team.

Our CTO at Kayak takes this a step further. He wants his entire team to *not* have industry experience. He believes this frees them from thinking like everyone else. It fosters a culture of constant creativity. He certainly has been successful following this path.

I preferred the best of both worlds. I hired fresh faces with passion and *no* industry knowledge and mixed them with experienced industry insiders who really knew travel.

This produced, shall we say, interesting results. The newbies and old-timers fought like cats in a bag, but that crucible produced wonderful results. In some cases, they understood the rationale and didn't change things. Other times, they threw bricks at the status quo and broke a lot of glass. I valued both results.

Rosabeth Moss Kanter of Harvard says, "Fresh thinking comes from fresh sources."[9] I believe she is spot-on. But mixing innovation with experience to engender debate can be useful.

Questions to Kick-Start Innovation

1. Do you have autonomy to select the members for your team vs. taking anyone who is "voluntold"? Explain.
2. What different levels of experience and varieties of expertise are on your team? Give examples.
3. How do you foster fresh thinking on your team?

Rock Stars Hang with Rock Stars

"The team with the best players wins."
—*Jack Welch, former CEO, General Electric*

"Rock star" employees are the best of the best. They are the ones that everyone raves about. If you hear about one, go get him or her.

Why? Because if you hire a rock star employee, other rock star employees will want to join the team. Rock star employees usually have great contact lists of other rock stars they like to work with. They understand that together they can produce exponential, rather than linear, output and outcomes.

I've seen this in action at Kayak.com. Our CTO recently told me the one thing he wished he'd learned earlier was "to spend more time hiring A players and less time trying to improve C players."

He works hard to find the best programmers out there. If he hears about one, he will run through walls to get the interview and convince him or her to come onboard. He willingly spends a great amount of time and energy because he knows high-performing employees attract people just like them who like to play on winning teams.

Hiring rock stars is one of the reasons Kayak.com has almost as many visitors as Travelocity.com, but only 5 percent of the employees!

To ensure we continue to have a winning team, Kayak uses a tough but effective practice. We force-rank employee performance and release a significant number of our bottom performers every year. This may seem harsh, but every company I know that does this (including us) reports that the remaining employees thank them.

Employees *know*, often more than senior management, who the poor performers are, and *they don't want to carry them.*

Releasing the bottom performers can be easier said than done. I once had an engineer who just could not make the transition to new technology. He'd been a great COBOL programmer, but his new code was buggy and slow, and his work was ranked at the bottom of the department. He was over forty, so HR told me I had to administer standardized tests to make sure he was incompetent. I did; he flunked. I knew he'd easily find a job writing COBOL somewhere else, so I asked, "Can I let him go now?"

HR said, "Nope. You need to send him to school for retraining." I deciding I was running a business, not a school for underperforming engineers, and fired him anyway. I got in "trouble," but the team thanked me, and we were more productive.

Salary and benefits are important, but people are more motivated by job satisfaction. Hire rock stars and don't keep the people who can only play piano at the Holiday Inn.

Questions to Kick-Start Innovation

1. Do you have a system for finding and hiring rock stars?
2. Do you have a policy about releasing your bottom performers?
3. Have you had to go to the mat to add a rock star to your team—or to fire an employee who was compromising effectiveness? What happened, and what were the results?

"This is Carl and Freda from Research & Development and over there is Daryl from our Crazy Dreamer Division."

Hire People Who Don't Fit In

*"The strength of the team is each individual member...
the strength of each member is the team."*
—*Phil Jackson, Los Angeles Lakers basketball coach*

We talked earlier about hiring a diverse mix of older, younger, experienced, and inexperienced people.

It's also important to hire people who don't fit in.

You want people who aren't like you. That might be a dorky programming genius or a *Mad Men* Don Draper marketing type in a tailored suit and tie.

The point is that you want people who won't agree with you. Smart people who challenge you, stretch you.

These people can be hard to manage, but it's usually worth it.

When I was running computer operations at American Airlines, business took a downturn, and I was required to reduce hundreds of staff. I told my data center manager he needed to lay off fifty people (a very sad and hard thing to do) and left him to it.

A week later, after reviewing the list of those affected, I asked, "Why did you fire John?"

"Well," came the reply, "he is a jerk and a slob. He doesn't follow the dress code, and he's always surly to me and the other supervisors. He just doesn't respect authority."

"All true," I replied, "but did you forget he saved us a million dollars by inventing a new front end for our system—something everyone else told us couldn't be done?"

My manager had forgotten that or chosen to ignore it. To him the guy was a jerk, enough reason to put him on the cut list.

Gordon Moore of Intel said, *"The world wants geniuses; it just wants them to behave like other people."*

Geniuses may not behave like other people, but they sure can produce fantastic results.

At one point, I worked in a small division at American that programmed and sold minicomputer accounting systems to travel agents. Our programming team was lead by a certified genius (Hugh) who had not a single social grace.

He was a huge man, six foot four and at least 350 pounds. His clothing was covered with stains from previous meals spattered all over.

His mind moved so fast that, in midsentence, he'd substitute the word "thing" for whatever he couldn't think of. For example, he'd say, "I'm going to replace that old program with 'thing,'" and expect us to figure it out.

But damn, was he smart. He made computers do things no one else could. He was flunking programming in college until a visiting professor noticed he was simply smarter than his instructor, who couldn't understand Hugh's code.

When we had to move our division to another town, Hugh announced he couldn't come, as he'd fallen in love with a topless dancer who was currently in jail for some minor offense.

Our chairman, who knew Hugh's value to the company, said, "I don't care if you have to hire F. Lee Bailey (the best lawyer in the United States at the time), get that stripper out of jail!"

Hire people who don't fit in and invest the time to manage them. Your team will benefit, and you will be well rewarded.

Questions to Kick-Start Innovation

1. Do you welcome people who don't fit in to your team? What's an example of someone who may not be the "norm," but has contributed to your organization?
2. Do you have people who don't agree with the company line, who bring up other points of view and perspectives? How does this pay off for your company?

Keep Teams Small

"Adding people to a late project will make it later!"
—Frederick Phillips Brooks, Jr., The Mythical Man-Month

Amazon has a great rule: "If it takes more than two pizzas to feed the team, the team is too big."

I agree. Teams charged with innovation need to be small. Team members need to sit together and interact all the time.

It's crucial to keep conversation flowing so challenges can be addressed and dealt with as they crop up.

Large teams have a lot of moving parts and require huge amounts of coordination. A large team simply lacks the cohesiveness, energy, and urgency of a smaller team. And if you want to give everyone a voice, it takes forever.

Large meetings face similar obstacles. At Kayak.com, we have "people counters" outside our meeting rooms to hold ourselves accountable for keeping meetings small...and productive.

Each person walking in has to push the button and increment the counter. The counter is there to remind us that once four or five people have entered, any more will create an ineffective meeting!

When I was running the SABRE system at American, it was time to add another computer to the four large ones that were running to capacity.

"It's too bad this last one will only be about 20 percent effective," one planner told me.

"How is that possible?" I asked.

"Well," came the answer, "it is going to spend most of its time communicating to the other four computers!"

Large teams and large meetings face the same problem. Remember, more people will not make things, as they say in Hawaii, "mo betta."

Questions to Kick-Start Innovation

1. Does your organization have a "two-pizza" team rule? How is that communicated and enforced?
2. How do you give team members an opportunity to have frequent face-to-face communication so they stay energized, focused, and on the same page?
3. If you need to work with a large team, what steps do you take to ensure they stay up to date, address challenges in the moment, and celebrate successes?

Can One Person Make a Difference?

"I've always tried to listen to everyone who works in the company.
I think that's more important than talking."
—Ken Feld, CEO, Ringling Brothers

Can one person really make a difference?

Sure. Think about Edison, Marconi, da Vinci, Einstein. They all made a difference...however, they didn't work in a company with layers of bureaucracy, committees, and red tape.

What about in your company? One person *can* make a difference *if you listen to them.*

We learned this the hard way at Travelocity. One employee at a competitor had an idea—*that got listened to*—that pushed us from being the number-one-ranked travel site to number two.

This employee was at Expedia. His idea was to allow customers to package air, car, and hotel together into a "dynamic package" and receive a discount. The new wrinkle was customers would receive the same types of discounts they could get on preplanned tours, but they got to select the components themselves instead of it being done for them.

This guy presented his idea to Expedia's president. He admitted it would cost a lot of money, take a long time, and there was no data to prove it would pay off. But he was convinced this was the next new thing, that it would be a revenue jackpot, and that it was important to get there first.

It took a year for this visionary (let's give him his due) to convince executives at Expedia they should try it, and many additional months to create the new option and make it real.

However, when they did put this new option in play, Expedia *doubled their sales in two quarters*. They passed Travelocity like we were stopped. We never caught up.

One guy. Just like the one guy who wouldn't give up at 3M and finally created the Post-it Note.

Maybe you're that one guy. Or maybe you're the decision maker who has one guy or gal on your team who is going to propose your industry's next new thing. Listen, and that one guy or gal might just supercharge your company.

Questions to Kick-Start Innovation

1. Who is someone in your organization who proposed a "radical" idea that ended up paying big dividends? How did that person finally get their idea approved?
2. How has that person's contribution paid off for your organization and changed the way you do business?
3. Who is someone on your team right now who is fighting for something new? How are you going to listen to that person and give his/her idea a chance?

Some People Will Leave as You Change...and That's OK

*"Never try to teach a pig to sing; it wastes
your time and it annoys the pig."*
—Paul Dickson, author

As you innovate your company, some people won't like or agree with what you're doing. They may vote with their feet and leave.

That's OK. That is probably good for you and good for them.

At Travelocity, we began with a group of risk takers. They were not conservative people who had their entire careers planned out, step by step. They were willing to try new things and understood failure is a necessary part of pioneering new products and services. They were the perfect group for our early days.

Five years later, many of them were gone. We'd grown to more than one thousand people, there were several layers of management, and we had become a big business. Some of those early hires hated it. So they left, and we replaced them with people who were better at *growing* a business than *starting* a business.

Travelocity recruited many mainframe programmers from American Airlines to help us build our software. We thought, "Well, they know the industry, and they know the complex airline pricing and ticketing systems; they should be the right people to help us."

A few were, but most simply could not adjust to the pace of web development. They wanted to work on yearlong projects, and they wanted to work nine to five. That just wasn't the way we operated. Many of them went back to AA.

Jay Walker, the founder of Priceline, had a theory about this. He told me once, "There are starters, growers, and runners. They are very different people. I want to create an environment where the starters can take a new company to one level and then return to start another one. I'll replace them with growers. And replace the growers with runners." Venture capitalists do much the same thing with their "entrepreneurs in residence" programs.

Jay's view has been borne out in my experience. I serve on several boards. I've seen CTOs lack the breadth to grow at the rapid pace of their company's expansion. I've seen CEOs continue to try to do everything themselves. If these executives aren't able to adapt their leadership style to match the changing needs of their position and organization, they need to be replaced.

"If you decide someone must go, don't procrastinate."[10] Almost always, you hang on too long, hoping the situation will improve. Usually it doesn't. So remember, it is OK for people to leave. Let them go or help them grow, but don't let them slow your organization's progress.

Questions to Kick-Start Innova

1. Is your company evolving? Are there employees who a along with the organization? How so?
2. How are you going to help them grow or let them go?

SECTION 3:

Create a Culture that Rewards Innovation

"I was successful because you believed in me."
—*Ulysses S. Grant*

Why Isn't Innovation Happening?

"Culture eats strategy for lunch."
—Dick Clark, Merck

It is important to remember that *you* don't have to be the one who comes up with all the great ideas. You just have to the one who creates an environment where everyone feels comfortable coming up with, and contributing, ideas.

If you've completely explained your vision, mission, strategies, and action plan to your employees, they are not the three blind mice wandering around in the dark.

If they understand the size of the opportunity, they should also understand they're part of the solution. If, for some reason, employees are not actively contributing ideas on how to do things better, faster, or cheaper...it's important to find out why.

Are they afraid they might innovate themselves out of a job? Are they reluctant to work on what appears to be a risky project? Are they afraid of being fired if this idea or program fails? Are they afraid your new strategy won't survive the next budget review... and their position will disappear right along with it?

While this book has sections about team, organizational structure, idea selection, and more, I believe the most important is *culture.*

You won't get anywhere if you don't create an environment where employees can let go of yesterday and grab on to tomorrow.

You won't progress unless you learn the fine art of killing projects, not people.

You won't succeed unless you and your team are willing to experiment and fail and try again...and try again.

This section offers twenty ideas to help you do all that.

Questions to Kick-Start Innovation

1. Do you know how *Webster's* dictionary defines "culture"?
   a) The quality in a person or society that arises from a concern for what is regarded as excellent in arts, manners, letters, or scholarly pursuits.
   b) Development or improvement of the mind by education or training.
   c) The behaviors and beliefs characteristic of a particular social, ethnic, or age group.
   d) The sum total of ways of living built up by a group of human beings and transmitted from one generation to another.
2. How would you define the culture in your organization?
3. What is the sum total of ways of living that have been built up by your group that are being transmitted to new hires?
4. What are the behaviors and beliefs characteristic of the people on your team and in your company?

Your Wake Is Larger Than You Imagine[11]

"In influencing others, example is not the main thing.
It is the only thing."
—*Albert Schweitzer*

It is important to remember that as you "motor" through your company—holding meetings, speaking to colleagues, giving presentations—you leave a big wake behind you.

That wake consists of *what* you say and, even more importantly, *how* you say it.

Employees have very sensitive antennae that detect (or think they detect) the hidden meaning behind everything you say. Their perception of your true intentions is what shapes their actions.

Do you support, amplify, and endorse new ideas?

Or, more often, do you find yourself minimizing, sidelining, and playing devil's advocate?

In your own mind, you see this as looking at new ideas from all angles to ensure their viability. But from your employees' point of view, it may seem you always shoot down what they say.

What you and your managers say, every day, matters a lot.

Although "walk the walk and talk the talk" has become a hackneyed phrase, it is crucial when building and sustaining an innovative culture.

During a rough economic patch at American, we were discussing cost cutting. To illustrate the point that small things can add up to big savings, our president told a group of VPs this story:

"I was on a flight the other day and noticed there were several olives in the salad I was served. I asked our food service director what each olive cost, and I was amazed to learn we spent $40,000 a year per olive. Figuring that no customer would complain about a missing olive, I ordered one removed!"

He set a wonderful example for us VPs to follow. Soon we were all searching for our "olive." What small cut could we make that would add up to big savings?

To ensure innovation will flourish in your company, watch your wake!

Questions to Kick-Start Innovation

1. If your employees or coworkers were asked how supportive you were of innovation, what would they say?
2. What is an example of how you actively support new ideas on how to do things better, faster, or cheaper?
3. Do you ever play devil's advocate? Is it possible this approach is being perceived as hypercritical? How can you look at ideas from all angles without discouraging employees from looking for their "olive"?

"It's always, 'Sit,' 'Stay,' 'Heel'--never 'Think,' 'Innovate,' 'Be yourself.'"

"The old tricks, young fellow, have served me well."

"We've Always Done It This Way"

"You've got to be original. If you're like everybody else,
what do they need you for?"
—*Bernadette Peters, actress, singer*

Anyone who has ever had a new idea has heard the dreaded words, *"But we've always done it this way."*

Those words just suck the air out of a room.

They are the stake in the heart of innovation.

Innovators must stand up to those words. People who are afraid of change say those words. People who want to keep things just the way they are. We don't move ahead by staying the way we are—we move ahead by being willing to do the new.

Unfortunately, many leaders want to keep the way it *was* the way it *is*. Why? Because it was *their* idea to be that way in the first place. They're invested in protecting and perfecting "the way it was" because it was their vision and they still want to be right.

So if you're going to challenge the way it *was*, you better come armed.

By armed, I mean armed with benchmarks. Armed with evidence and precedence of where your idea has worked elsewhere. Armed with the support of influential individuals who believe your proposed idea is a calculated risk worth taking.

In the past few years, many large insurance companies have hired me to speak at their annual meetings. They see the parallel between the demise of travel agents and the current state of insurance agents and want to get ahead of that curve. Some want to eliminate agents. Some want to ensure their agents survive in an industry that is rapidly eliminating anyone with the title "agent." Either path can succeed, but at least they see the threat and understand they need to adapt, and adapt fast.

Good for them for being proactive, not passive. Many established companies view disruption as a threat, not an opportunity. They try to protect the status quo rather than saying, "How can we adapt?" or, more importantly, "How can we use our unique attributes to be even better than those new guys?"

The Internet is accelerating economic Darwinism.

Access to perfect information on product, price, and availability is dooming the middleman. It is quickly creating the "frictionless" commerce that Bill Gates predicted in the mid '90s.

I was lucky at AA to have a boss who understood the forces of change could work for you or against you. An innovator himself, he almost always stood on the side of moving forward and facilitating change rather than fighting it.

When someone proposed selling our yield management software to other airlines, most of us were aghast, as it was key in those days to our revenue superiority. The marketing department in particular was vigorous in its opposition.

But our president, Bob Crandall, said, *"Well, somebody is going to copy this software and make a lot of money, so it might as well be us!"* He reserved the crown jewels of the code for our company, but allowed the sale of the rest.

"Someone will do this, so it might as well be us" thinking can be a helpful piece of ammunition when fighting naysayers.

Another way to turn a potential no into a green light is to say, "Let's try this on a small scale and see how it works." A smaller ask can make it easier to say yes.

When presenting a new idea, ask yourself if the decision maker has a vested interest in protecting the status quo. If so, make sure to come armed with documentation of exactly how this idea is going to produce bottom-line results for the organization. By making your arguments objective, not subjective, the decision maker is more likely to embrace the idea rather than ignore it.

Questions to Kick-Start Innovation

1. Have you ever proposed a new idea and been told, "But we've always done it this way"? How did that impact your willingness to suggest new ideas from then on?

2. Do you have an idea on how your current organization could be more effective? How can you arm yourself with objective evidence showing how this will contribute to the bottom line? What support can you get to motivate your decision maker to embrace this idea, not ignore it?

Innovation Is Like Baseball, Not the Olympics

"Success isn't permanent, and failure isn't fatal."
—Mike Ditka

Innovation is not like the Olympics.

In the Olympics, you train from when you are eight 'til you are eighteen. You get one six-minute run down the mountain, one nine-second race, one attempt at a vault. You finish out of the medals or come in fourth. Your dreams are dashed, and your life is over!

Innovation is more like baseball. You can fail 70 percent of the time and actually be considered quite good.

There's another analogy from baseball that applies to innovation. *Most games are won with singles and doubles, not home runs.*

Home runs are great. They are that 10 percent of innovation that is transformational, exciting, and extremely rewarding.

But the 70 percent of innovation that generally involves changes to your core products and the 20 percent that represents adjacent changes are just as important.

At Kayak, we are constantly searching for "singles" and "doubles" that can improve our purchase conversion even a few basic points.

Most innovation is about small changes to your core product, pricing model, or service delivery.

Every once in a while, it's exciting to swing for the fences, but don't forget, lots of singles and doubles can win games, too.

Questions to Kick-Start Innovation

1. What is a small change to your core product, pricing model, or service delivery that proved to be a winner?
2. What system do you have in place for rewarding "singles" and "doubles" to encourage employees to suggest what may initially seem like a small idea?

Experiment!

*"When you lose, you have to figure out what you did,
what you didn't do, and what you want to do next time
you're in that situation...and then go do it."*
—*Jack Nicklaus, champion golfer*

Experimentation is the key to success in innovation. You're rarely going to hit the target the first time. However, each time you don't hit the target, you can analyze what went wrong and figure out how to get closer each time until...bull's-eye!

One of the great beauties of the online world is you can experiment and get feedback so quickly. Formal focus groups have become outmoded because they can't compete with the instant answers we can get by testing online.

If you've watched the Emmy Award–winning TV show *Mad Men*, you've learned that the ad business has copywriters and editors. The copywriters come up with the ads, and the editors pick the best. So be an editor for a minute. Take a look at these four ads.

Which would you select as the best? Even though they have almost the same words, same colors, and same layout, the one on the bottom left generated 35 percent more revenue than the other three!

How did the organization pick the right ad? They tested all four, online, for one hour and picked the highest scorer. That is the value of online experimentation.

At Kayak.com, about 20 percent of our visitors see an experiment every day. We base our future actions on the results. It's not that customers tell us what to build; they just tell us what they like the best, which helps us strategize what are the best features to include.

In your company, everyone will have an opinion about how products should be designed and what features they should have. Their opinions matter, but keep in mind it is what your *customers* select that matters most. Measurement, using customer-driven data to direct changes, and being OK with trial and error are your keys to successful experimentation.

Questions to Kick-Start Innovation

1. Do you experiment online to receive feedback from customers as to what they like/don't like, buy/don't buy?
2. Do you use this customer-driven data to drive innovation? How so?

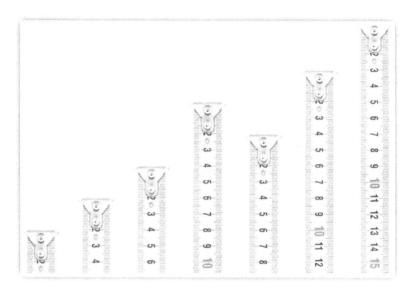

Measure

"Measure twice, cut once."
—American proverb

The key to successful experimentation is measurement. It sounds simple, but you've got to remove opinion from the results and stick to the data.

I've sat in on dozens of focus groups. I've carefully watched customers interact with products and have heard many differing opinions about why the customers acted the way they did.

In the end, those opinions were just subjective interpretations.

All that mattered in the long run was the careful documentation of customer answers to specific questions. That's what leads to genuine, often unexpected insight.

My favorite story, probably apocryphal, about focus groups and usability testing is about an AOL user who was brought in to test an early version of Google.

After being presented with Google's very simple search box, she simply sat there for several minutes, doing nothing.

Focus group overseers are *not* supposed to intervene, but one couldn't help himself. He broke protocol and asked, "What are you waiting for?"

As she was a longtime AOL user, probably still using very slow dial-up for her Internet connection, she replied, *"I'm waiting for the rest of the screen to paint."*

Remember this the next time you introduce something revolutionary. You may receive negative responses or wildly enthusiastic responses. What's important is to understand and document *why* your customers are responding the way they do.

At Travelocity, we spent thousands of hours trying to discover why, of the millions of customers who came to our home page, only 3–4 percent would purchase.

That isn't a bad score for an online business, but we always tried to emphasize to our team the dramatic difference a small increase in that rate, even .05 percent, could have for our company.

Our logic was that we'd already spent marketing dollars to get customers to our site. We'd already expended most of our costs by the time they searched for available flights. So if we could get customers to buy one, it was all profit.

One time, several customers called to tell us they'd booked with Travelocity, and when they got to the airport, there was no record of their reservation. They were rightfully very angry.

Because we saved every single search they'd made, we were able to track their path through the website. We discovered these customers were clicking on a new feature that let them review their itinerary before completing their booking. As they could see the details of the reservation before their eyes, they thought they were finished and happily logged off to do something else. If we hadn't saved their searches, we never would have found the problem. Nor would we have been able to use the accumulated knowledge of customer problems to improve our site and steadily raise our conversion rate over time.

It's said, "If you can't measure it, you can't manage it." I believe that if you don't measure it, you can't *improve* it. The average retail online conversion is 3–4 percent. Yet L. L. Bean is at an impressive 18 percent, and Lillian Vernon is at an amazing 20 percent.

Part of this is because we are all dedicated to experimenting and measuring as the surest path to improvement. We test, measure, modify…test, measure, modify…forever!

Questions to Kick-Start Innovation

1. What systems do you have in place for testing, measuring, and modifying?
2. What's an example of how you've used your measured data to improve your conversion, sales, and profits?

Allow Failure—Harvest Learning

"At Intuit we allow failure and harvest learning."
—*Scott Cook, founder Intuit*

Do you celebrate failure as well as success? Well, if you don't celebrate it, do you at least learn from it?

In some companies, failure is buried. It is talked about in hushed tones, and the program leader is quickly transferred to the company's version of Siberia.

At Grey Advertising, they have a "Heroic Failure Award." They present it to one person each year who, in their opinion, tried the hardest...and still failed. They know you need to dissect failure just like you do success.

Sports teams fanatically analyze every aspect of losing games with the same process and vigor they use for winning ones. The

FAA has a painstaking process for analyzing every airline incident and crash. As a result, their safety record gets better every year. Your quality department surely uses fishbone diagrams to analyze every part of your manufacturing process to search out and destroy defects. Why not employ that process to innovation?

We did something similar at Travelocity. If we had a bad implementation, we'd perform a code and process review to find the error. We were careful to communicate and correct the error constructively. We'd gather the project team and some "wise ones" (respected longtime employees) to discuss what happened.

We established guidelines in the first few minutes of the meeting. Finger pointing and blaming were not allowed. Our goal was to find solutions, not fault. We'd inspect the process, find the defect, and strategize how to make it better.

Obviously, if the *same* people kept making the *same* mistakes, we'd arrange for them to get counseling, training…or, eventually, be put on the bus out of town. But that was rare; the focus was on identifying errors, not on identifying blame.

Employees often assume that messengers of bad news will be shot. I know this firsthand. I once fired an employee who single-handedly took our entire SABRE system down for almost twenty-four hours. He confessed he had *deliberately ignored process,* but some employees thought he was being punished for making a mistake anyone could have made.

I had to work very hard against the rumor mill to clarify that he was fired *not* because he made a mistake, but because he knowingly violated a written process, with disastrous results. It took lots of work to set this straight, but it was worth it.

Questions to Kick-Start Innovation

1. Do you have a "work the process, not the people" approach when dealing with mistakes? How so?
2. What guidelines do you set when discussing errors so the focus is on finding solutions, not fault?

Make New Mistakes

"Boy, was that a wrong mistake."
—Yogi Berra

We've talked about the importance of making mistakes. Let's clarify that.

It's important to make mistakes (to fail while trying). If you don't, you are not trying hard enough. At Travelocity, our mantra, as an old colleague reminded me the other day, was "Make new mistakes." We knew we might fail, but we wanted to ensure we learned from those failures, and if we were to fail again (and we certainly were), to ensure that failure was something that had never happened before.

Pioneers don't have anyone to emulate. We were our own scout. We knew we'd fail; we just made sure each failure was a first-time failure that hadn't happened before. It wasn't comfortable. But it sure was exhilarating, and ultimately very successful.

Questions to Kick-Start Innovation

1. How do you emphasize in your organization that mistakes are welcome… as long as they're *new* mistakes?
2. Are you pioneering a new industry? Acting as your own scout? How do you encourage first-time failures?

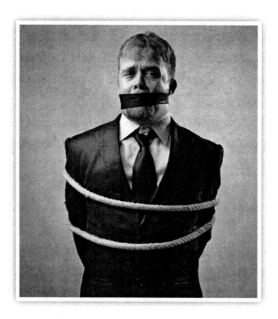

Kill the Project, Not the Person

"I'm always blown away by the fact that, in some companies, everybody can say no and nobody can say yes. Saying yes takes a leap of faith."
—*Ronald Shaich, Panera Bread*

In the early days of Travelocity, when the web was still based on very slow dial-up, we decided to create a CD-ROM that featured colorful video footage of the Caribbean. Our logic was that the more people could see videos of the beach, palm trees, and plush resorts, the more they'd want to go there and the more packages they'd buy.

We hired a production and marketing firm and spent a million dollars getting that CD-ROM to the stores. A few months later, our paltry sales figures made it clear this idea was going nowhere.

I had to go to my boss, the former CFO of American Airlines and no financial pushover, and tell him I'd lost a million bucks. I have to tell you, I was not looking forward to this.

He listened to my tale of woe and said, *"Well, Terry, what did you learn?"*

Word of that conversation spread like wildfire. Not only had I not been fired, demoted, or chastised, but he made it clear he'd continue to support experimentation, even if the resulting innovation didn't pay off.

I can only imagine how easy it would have been for him to say no to pricy experimentation happening on his watch. Instead, his yes sent a clear message that he didn't just *say* he worked the process and not the people, he meant it and did it.

I knew I couldn't lose a million bucks again, but I also knew he had my back.

Bosses who support creative problem solving perpetuate it. One of my favorite examples of this happened at American Airlines.

A snowstorm had paralyzed the Denver airport. Our station manager was unable to get our airplane plowed out of a large drift. We only had one gate, and all the plows were working on United and Continental, who practically owned the airport. The manager asked airport control for help, to no avail. He couldn't find anyone to hire or any plows to rent to open his station, so he got creative. He bought a brand new truck that came equipped with a snowplow from a local dealer. He charged it to his expense account and dug out the airplane himself.

Our president not only paid the bill, he promoted the manager for his initiative! Executives who reward initiative get more of it.

Questions to Kick-Start Innovation

1.   Has someone in your organization taken a big, calculated risk that didn't pay off? What happened?

Leverage Your Strengths

"The real difficulty in changing the course of any enterprise lies not in developing new ideas, but in escaping from old ones."
—*John Maynard Keynes*

Experimentation and measurement let you "fail fast," because you're getting the feedback you need to make adjustments.

However, even if data indicate no one is using your new product or service, you might want to keep tweaking instead of abandoning your innovation efforts and assume all is lost.

There is a story about Amazon that illustrates this idea. In its early years, Amazon was envious of the success eBay was having with their auctions. So they tried auctions and failed. eBay was also doing well with stores, so Amazon tried that, too, and failed.

Finally, they stepped back and asked themselves, "What is different between our two companies?"

They decided that since Amazon was a community of book lovers (obviously this was before they started selling everything from bats to boats), perhaps they should play to that strength.

Brainstorming around their core customer and competency led them to consider selling *used* books.

That was a big leap of faith, as there are very few businesses (other than autos) that sell used and new versions of the same product in the same store. However, there were many attractive attributes to selling used books:

- They didn't have to acquire the books.
- They didn't have to store the books.
- They didn't have to pick, pack, and ship the books.
- The margins were almost equal to selling new books.

To make this a success, they had to "fail fast," *and* they had to escape from the preconceived notion that you couldn't purchase used and new items in the same store.

Sometimes a radical new idea will force you to create a new organization (as Amazon did with its cloud computing business). But sometimes your radical new idea is sitting smack dab in the middle of what you are currently doing…and *you* have to change to accept it.

Is your organization playing to its strengths? Have you identified your core competency and core customer? Are you leveraging them by experimenting with innovative products and services that will help you continue to be their first choice, best choice, and only choice?

Questions to Kick-Start Innovation

1. What would *you* say is your organization's strength?
2. What would your employees and coworkers say is your organization's strength?

IDEA 27

Prepare if You Cross the Valley of Death!

"I will fear no evil."
—Psalms 23:4

Change is hard, and moving a large company in a new direction…
well, that's very hard.

In one of the companies I work with, revenue was shrinking.
Competitors had replaced our product with better and faster models, but for a variety of reasons we couldn't replicate their offering.
It was clear we'd have to change.

The company came up with a series of ideas for new, adjacent
products. Many of them made use of our core strengths. But no matter which ones we selected, it was going to be a long slog, filled with
great risk to change the company's direction, customers, and culture.

At a meeting where the new ideas were presented, most were excited by the future, and we selected the winners and planned to move forward.

After the vote, I said, "I'm very happy we've made these choices. I think they are the right ones for the company. But in moving from here to there, we are going to have to cross the 'Valley of Death.'"

The CEO, shocked, looked at me and said, "What do you mean by that?"

"Well," I replied, "it's much like *Crossing the Chasm*, but worse. We're not a start-up; we're a public company. We not only have to take our cash and create our new products, we have to keep our shareholders believing in us, and we have to run our old business at the same time to keep the dollars coming in. It is going to be very, very hard. I believe we can do it, but I want everyone to be realistic about how hard this change will be. We will have to cross Death Valley to get to the Promised Land."

The room was silent.

The CEO adjourned the meeting, and the troops filed out. Then he said, "I am very upset at what you said, and I don't want you talking that way to my people again."

"OK," I replied, "but I hope you will at least consider how hard this will be. Some of our ideas will fail, and perhaps only one will succeed. We have to be ready for that."

I held my tongue in future meetings, but the plan played out as I expected. In fact, all of the new products failed.

Innovation isn't easy, it doesn't always work, and you have to change. Some pioneers did make it across Death Valley, and they got to live in California. It can work out well. But take a lot of water, keep everyone in the wagons, and move fast!

Questions to Kick-Start Innovation

1. Will your innovation push you across the Valley of Death?
2. How can you support ideas in the best way for success?

IDEA 28

Eyes Wide Shut

*"I'll **see** it when I **believe** it."*
—*Anonymous*

When giving a PowerPoint presentation, have you ever had to search for a binder or something (anything!) to put under the projector to tilt it up so the images hit the screen?

How is it possible the manufacturers of these projectors haven't fixed this design flaw? I'm not an engineer, but I can think of at least three ways to make projectors tilt correctly.

Perhaps the screens at the manufacturer's test facilities are perfectly positioned on the walls so the images show up in the center of the screen, every time, all the time. Maybe the designers have never had to walk into a hotel ballroom and deliver a keynote presentation to a thousand business owners who are wondering why you keep fiddling with the projector (as it falls off the stack of books you borrowed to prop it up…again).

Or maybe they just have their "eyes wide shut" and don't see their products from the eyes of their customers.

I've stayed in dozens of hotels where the desk chairs were made for midgets, the soap was wrapped in impenetrable plastic, and the shower controls were inscrutable. Would that really happen if the managers actually used the hotel?

How could the maker of this parking meter have missed how confusing their opening message is: *"Press CANCEL to begin."*

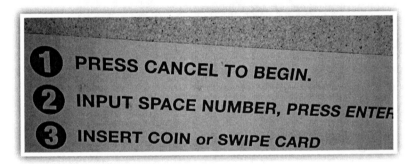

On the other hand, when British Airways decided to revolutionize their first-class cabin, they hired a designer who specialized in yachts. They (accurately) predicted that anyone who could build luxury into the small confines of a boat could do the same for a plane.

The president of British Airways then test-marketed that innovation with his team. He had their first-of-its-kind "bedlike" seats assembled at a London warehouse and arranged for his executives to eat meals and spend a couple of nights sleeping in them! Adjustments were made based on their real-life experience; only then were they ready to be used by customers.

Questions to Kick-Start Innovation

1. What processes do you have in place to help you experience your products through the eyes of customers?
2. How do you test your innovations with your employees before launch?

Should You Bet the Farm on Your Intuition?

"Intuition is simply the sum of all your experience!"
—Kip Tindell

Is it OK to go with your gut when you're innovating?

Sure. Just don't bet the farm on it.

Sometimes, as leaders, we feel sure our vision is correct.

We're convinced our idea is the best. We believe our intuition is infallible.

And perhaps it is. But since it is as likely as not that your gut isn't a mortal lock (remember, most experiments fail initially), why take a chance?

We will talk more specifically about prototypes in Idea 57, but the beauty of prototyping today is you can get instant feedback at low cost over the net.

Even physical models can be "built" through images, videos, or created with a 3-D printer and evaluated to get user input.

By all means, listen to your intuition and instincts. Check in with your gut. Ask yourself what feels right.

Then mitigate the risk of banking on your intuition by:

- Experimenting and monitoring feedback, traffic, and buying patterns from customers.
- Building a prototype and testing it in a lab.
- Tweaking your innovation based on the information you receive.

When you've done the above and have evidence that your innovation will work…then bet the farm on it!

"I like making decisions with intuition. I like to validate with analytics," says Jeff Hsun Huang Nvidia.[12]

Questions to Kick-Start Innovation

1. What role do you feel intuition and gut instincts play in making good decisions? What's an example of when you followed your gut and it paid off for you?
2. How does your organization integrate feelings and facts when producing innovative products and services—so it's not an either/or situation, it's the best of both worlds?

Naysayers Suck

"Negative people are energy vampires."
—*Jim Marsicano, general manager, Travelocity*

My colleague, Jim, was spot-on. Negativity kills innovation.

I received an e-mail from someone who had attended one of my speeches. She said, "I was so excited after your speech and started changing things in my department. I told a couple of my colleagues what I was doing, and they immediately brought me down. All they could talk about was why this wouldn't work. I wasn't sure they attended the same presentation!"

We've all met people like this. The naysayers, the glass-half-empty people, are the enemies of innovation.

As Tachi Yamada of the Gates Foundation put it, "The biggest problems I see in a group of people who don't embrace change is that they will always fight anything new, any new idea, any new concept, any outside point of view. And there are many examples of companies that have filed for bankruptcy because of that."[13]

Hold negative people accountable for their criticism! Instead of allowing them to carp about why an idea *won't* work, ask them to come up with ways it *could* work.

If people are afraid of change because there's been a history of unsupported innovation and they're afraid for their job, educate them about your "kill the project, not the person" approach.

However, if someone always seems to walk around with a rain cloud over their head and seems to revel in the role of being the team naysayer, find something else for them to do.

Bottom line? Habitual critics, naysayers, and "mean people" consume energy and impetus. Get them off your innovative project before they suck the life right out of it.

Questions to Kick-Start Innovation

1. Have you been on a team that had a habitual naysayer on it? How did that person impact that group?
2. How did the leader deal with this individual so that he or she didn't undermine the innovation culture?
3. Is there someone in your group right now who is sucking the energy and impetus from your project? How are you going to hold that person accountable for contributing instead of constantly criticizing?

Quality vs. Speed

*"One doesn't discover new lands without consenting
to lose sight of the shore for a very long time."*
—Andre Gide

A few years ago, I was invited to make a speech on innovation for the American Association of Quality Management.

I initially wondered if I was the right person for this job. How does one talk about innovation to *quality* professionals?

Quality professionals insist on everything being perfect before it is shipped. They're reluctant to approve projects unless all processes have been locked in and locked down. They're often perceived as conservatives who are unwilling to take risks, while innovators eat risk for lunch.

As a result, organizational innovation often ends up being a tug-of-war between the quality folks and the project creators.

I thought about it some more and realized how wrong I was.

First of all, the worldwide quality movement has resulted in higher quality products with few, if any, design flaws. The quality movement has improved processes and lowered costs. Secondly, while the software industry can ship buggy products and call them "beta," airplane manufacturers can't do that, nor can automakers or NASA. Don't even think about giving our astronauts a beta space suit...

So we are indebted to quality professionals for the pivotal role they've played in advancing innovation.

That became the theme of my presentation to AAQM. I was honest, though, in letting the audience know that I believe focusing on quality *too early* in the ideation process can hobble innovation.

That's why I'm such a proponent of prototypes and customer-tested beta experiments and measurements.

Quality processes need to be developed before a product is ready to ship. Quality tools like fishbone diagrams can help take a product from a buggy test to a deliverable.

However, I asked these quality professionals to honor the need for the "throw it against the wall" free-thinking process that is so crucial at the beginning stages of innovation.

I closed by requesting they save the detailed-oriented mind-set, also necessary to the process, for *after* the trial-and-error prototypes and experimentation have been given the opportunity to play their role in the innovation game.

Make sure you bring quality in at the right time of the ideation process.

Questions to Kick-Start Innovation

1. Do you have quality professionals who work in, or consult with, your organization? What role do they play?
2. At what stage are quality professionals brought into the innovation process, and what authority do they have?
3. Do you have a policy or procedure for how you balance the need and timing for detailed "quality" requirements with the need for experimentation? What is that?

When You're in a Maze, You May Need a Chainsaw

"Society bristles with enigmas which look hard to solve."
—*Honoré de Balzac*

Have you ever tried to find your way through a maze?

If you're patient, have a great memory, and don't mind trial and error, you can eventually find an elegant way out.

Sometimes, though, if you've been in a maze too long and you don't know which way to go—or you're going in circles—you've got to get decisive, grab a chainsaw, and cut yourself out.

And yes, this is a metaphor. Companies sometimes create byzantine mazes you need to cut your way through to get anything innovative out the door and on its way.

The precursor to Travelocity, EAASY SABRE, was the main travel booking site on CompuServe, Prodigy, and AOL for many years. We felt hemmed in by the strong design criteria of these portals and their insistence that they knew travel and design better than we did. (Why did they hire us again?)

We eventually lost the AOL account, but when we launched Travelocity, we wanted it back, as we were fighting Microsoft's Expedia and needed all the help we could get.

We won the business and then set out (on our own) to redesign the service. We thought about making incremental changes, but in our hearts, we knew the AOL design was a failure.

Rather than working through the maze, we took out our chainsaw and just cut our way out!

We threw out the cluttered look and focused the user on making the booking. It was a radical departure from what AOL had had for years, but we believed it was the best way to move forward.

We traveled to their HQ to present it and held our breath.

"Wow, that's a very big change," they said. "It certainly is a departure from what we'd do, but you guys are the experts. Let's give it a try."

That innovation increased their sales 40 percent the first day!

Sometimes you have to take a chainsaw to the maze.

Questions to Kick-Start Innovation

1. Are you in the midst of an innovation and feel you're in a complicated maze that is slowing the process? Explain.
2. Is it time to get out your chainsaw? Why so?
3. What radical departure from the norm do you think is called for to move your project forward?

Are You Running Around with Your Hair on Fire?

"You're not going to be happy unless
you're going Mach 2 with your hair on fire."
—Top Gun

I recently spoke to two hundred of the top leaders of a multibillion-dollar company. I kicked off the day with my speech on building digital relationships, as this was a company that knew it had to change how it distributed its products.

Later in the day, I gave my innovation speech and then attended their breakout sessions to help in their brainstorming. It was clear from the discussions that this was a company that needed to change and knew it.

At the end of the day, the chairman of the company got up and summarized the meeting. He reminded everyone how well the company was doing in many areas and cautioned them with, "Now, don't run around with your hair on fire innovating everything!" He exhorted them to focus on the few areas he thought needed improvement.

You could feel the energy drain out of the room.

I understood where he was coming from. He didn't want people to willy-nilly start changing anything and everything.

But by saying *what* he said and *when* he said it, I believe he seriously undermined the purpose of their meeting.

Remember Idea 18, where we talked about the wake you leave?

There is absolutely a time and place to focus efforts. But if the goal is to inspire employees to be more innovative, a few "hair burning" days might be in order.

A few years ago, I was asked to speak on innovation to a 150-year-old company. I wasn't quite sure how to do this. I mean, they'd been around 150 years; maybe they had it down?

Before the meeting, I talked to employees at the reception. I asked one woman how innovation was going in their company. "Oh," she said, "I've just done something really innovative."

"Cool, what was that?" I asked.

"Well, I have fixed all our Adobe-based application forms so customers can fill them out online rather than printing them out and having to fill them in by hand."

"That's great, I'm sure your customers will love that," I said. I chose not to tell her this idea had been around so long that *even the IRS* changed to fill-in Adobe forms five years before.

The point? People have their own perspectives. That *was* a "hair on fire" innovation for her and her department, and it did move their 150-year-old company in the right direction. Good for her.

Questions to Kick-Start Innovation

1. Are there mixed messages in your organization about innovation? Do they encourage you one moment and tell you not to "run around with your hair on fire" the next?
2. How can you honor people's personal perspectives about what constitutes innovation so they feel supported?

A Twenty-Year Overnight Success

*"To do disruptive innovation, you have to be willing
to be misunderstood for a very long time."*
—*Jeff Bezos, Amazon.com*

When you hear about successful start-ups, sometimes it seems they're an overnight success. Sometimes that is true; mostly not.

Yes, Instagram went from nothing to a billion-dollar sale in one year. But Facebook, at this writing, is ten years old and just now went public.

Travelocity actually evolved from an earlier product called EAASY SABRE. EAASY SABRE was almost eight years old when I was put in charge of the product (for the second time).

We changed that old product dramatically and put it on the Internet. It took off, but even though growth was superfast, we didn't go public for five years and it took us seven to be profitable.

So it took us a total of thirteen years to go from conception to a public, profitable company.

And remember, along the way, there was no guaranteed outcome. We had to keep scouting our way.

My point is, even though you need to have the flexibility to "fail fast," you also need to stay on your core idea's course.

When Travelocity went public, many of our investor meetings received "polite interest." Travel was just not the hot topic then.

Investors were excited about Pets.com, eToys, and Webvan—categories they were *sure* would be big. (Remember them?)

Thankfully, we (and SABRE) were more interested in building a company than in building a stock.

In a very short period of time, *travel became the largest part of e-commerce.* It is so big that most studies leave it out of the graph of e-commerce growth as it distorts the curve.

It is larger than the next four categories of e-commerce combined! Take books, movies, electronics, apparel…there is nothing to touch it. The pundits were completely wrong.

So as you experiment, don't waver from the core proposition and energizing concept that got you excited in the first place. Yes, you've got to fail fast on features, tweaks, and improvements. And you may have to pivot on the revenue plan, how you get customers, and how you roll out. But if you want to be an "overnight success" (even if it takes twenty years), be willing to persevere through the ups and down of you being one of the few who see the potential of your innovation.

Questions to Kick-Start Innovation

1. Are you part of a company that's viewed as an "overnight success"? How long did it actually take to break out?
2. What's one of your favorite examples of an organization that persevered through the ups and down over the years to have dramatic success?

IDEA 35

The Beach Ball Effect

*"Every truth has two sides; it is as well to
look at both before we commit ourselves to either."*
—Aesop

The big picture doesn't just come from distance or time; it also comes from looking at an issue from all sides.

The Beach Ball Effect is what happens when two or more people are on different sides of the ball; they can only see the colors on their side. They may assume the other side is a mirror image of theirs or assume it is different. They can guess what's over there, but they can't know unless they look all around the ball.

Ideas are like beach balls. I'm thinking about the idea one way, and you're thinking about it another. Unless we look at all sides, unless we really talk it out, we can leave with very different impressions of what the idea is all about!

The longtime CIO at American (and a great mentor to me) was Max Hopper. He had a wonderfully innovative mind. He was both great and sometimes frustrating to report to.

Some days he'd get up at the white board and talk and draw and we'd be mesmerized. What he was saying was so interesting! Then he'd say, "Well, go off and get started." As we walked out the door, we would realize we had no clue what to do.

I'd come back and stare at that white board. Sometimes I'd get what he was driving at, and I'd run off to get going. Other times, it was just impenetrable. But that is exactly what innovation and working with very smart people is like!

Max taught me about the Beach Ball Effect, but he didn't call it that. We learned to call him "Micro Max" or "Macro Max." We never knew which Max we'd meet when we came in the door.

If your pitch tried to paint the macro picture of the industry and the broad stokes of your idea, just to gauge his interest, he'd nail you with questions on the tiniest details of your concept. "What about this? What about that?" If you hadn't thought it all out, he'd send you away to get that done.

If you came in with a one-hundred-page deck, having spent months on determining every detail, he'd close the deck after a few pages, look you in the eye, and say, "Well, let's talk about the big picture here." You couldn't win. But in a way, it was always a win.

All he was really doing was making sure we'd looked all around the beach ball. He wanted to ensure we'd forced our thinking to see how the idea would fit into our market and the world, *and* that we'd sweated all the details before we began. It was frustrating, but many times it kept our new idea out of the ditch.

Be sure to see *all* the sides of the beach ball of your idea.

Questions to Kick-Start Innovation

1. Do you agree that ideas are like beach balls? How so?

It's All about Follow-Through

"Thousands of people have talent. I might as well congratulate you for having eyes in your head. The one and only thing that counts is: do you have staying power?"
—Noel Coward

At a dude ranch recently, I learned ax throwing.

Yes, you read that right. I discovered pretty quickly that hitting the target (as you can see in the photo on the top of the page) really is *all* about follow-through. When I didn't remember to follow through, I missed every time.

The same is true in innovation. Remember, innovation is about putting ideas to work. It is not enough to be creative enough and have an idea. You have to work out how to build it, raise the money, get it out in the world, market it, and create excitement for it. If you don't, it isn't innovation; it is just a nice, dusty idea.

Hanging on the wall of my office, I have a plaque of one of the patents I've been issued. I'm proud of that patent. Unfortunately, that is all that was created from the idea. A patent. The product was never built. It remains an idea, not a product. It's creative, but it is not an innovation.

Comedian Judy Tenuta said, "My parents told me I wouldn't amount to anything because I procrastinated so much. I told them, 'Just you wait.'"

Nike has it right: don't procrastinate, don't wallow in excuses, don't get waylaid by naysayers, *just do it*.

Questions to Kick-Start Innovation

1. Do you have an innovative idea that you're going to propose…someday? What are you waiting for?
2. Did you launch an innovative project…but haven't followed through? Why?
3. What incentive can you give yourself and your team to motivate you to fight the good fight and turn your idea into a real-world innovation that adds value for you and your organization?

SECTION 4:

Generate More Ideas, Better Ideas

"The best way to have a good idea is to have lots of ideas."
—*Linus Pauling*

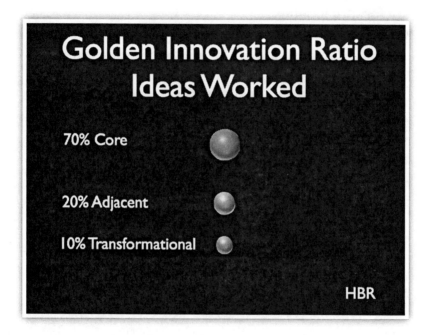

The Golden Ratio of Innovation

"There's a way to do it better—find it."
—Thomas Edison

The graph above is the Golden Ratio of Innovation.[14]

As you begin to generate new ideas for new products, you would do well to keep this ratio in mind.

Companies that are most successful with innovation follow this ratio, and they are rewarded by Wall Street for doing so. Companies that follow this ratio have a higher price/earnings ratio than those that don't.

Spending 70 percent of your research and development dollars on improving your core is conservative and makes investors happy and calm. Spending the remaining 30 percent on adjacent and transformational projects doesn't scare anyone and seems like you are forward looking.

But before you settle on this, you should know that the *revenue* that accrues from innovation has quite a different graph.

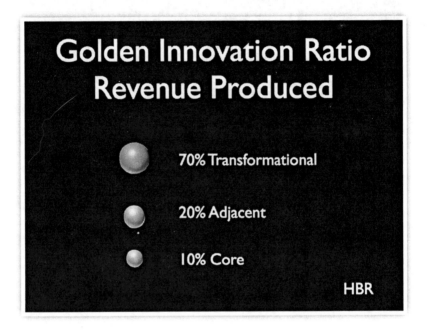

As you can see, *the majority of the revenue comes from your transformational ideas.*

These are the radical, hard-to-manage, out-of-the-box, crazy ideas that make you uncomfortable.

And they only make up 10 percent of your innovation efforts. But because they are the big wins, they must be managed most carefully of all!

The core changes usually come easily to mind, and, as discussed, many of them come from customers. It is the transformational ones that are hard to think up and, more importantly, hard to push ahead against the organizational pressure that finds them foolish, impossible, or threatening. However, it's crucial to keep the "crazy" ideas in the mix, because, to paraphrase Willie Sutton, "That's where the money is."

Questions to Kick-Start Innovation

1. What percentage of your R&D dollars is spent on improving your core products and services?
2. What percentage is spent on adjacent/transformational projects and radical, crazy, game-changing ideas?
3. Have you tracked your *revenue* from innovation?

Would Your Company Approve
the Idea that Formed It?

*"Yes, risk taking is inherently failure prone.
Otherwise, it would be called 'sure-thing taking.'"*
—Jim McMahon

Think about the risks that were taken by those who formed your organization.

Would the culture of FedEx today approve an idea as crazy as getting anything delivered in the United States "absolutely, positively, overnight"? (There is a tale that founder Fred Smith's college professor gave him a C grade for that idea.)

Have you heard of Digital Equipment Corporation? Thought not. It was started when founder Ken Olsen noticed students preferred small, real-time computers to the faster, bigger, but batch-oriented, IBM machines. He thought (correctly) that real-time minicomputers would be the next big thing. At its height, Digital Equipment Corporation had one hundred thousand employees and was the second largest computer company in the United States. Yet Olsen missed the next wave, famously saying, "There is no reason for any individual to have a computer in his home." The moral of that story? DEC no longer exists.

Think back to when your company was created. Think about the economy, business environment, and how risky the core idea for this company probably was, but they decided to do it anyway.

Does your company today have enough of an innovative culture to take that daring of a risk? Would you?

If you go to an observatory and look at a supernova, you are watching something that happened perhaps millions of years ago. That star may be long gone, snuffed out before we existed: but you can *still* see the image from Earth.

Some companies are the same way, still running on a big-bang idea created many years ago. But how long will the light from that star last?

We've already talked about some of the products and services (i.e., records/CDs) that have disappeared or been radically altered since the Internet came on the scene. Here are some more.

- Newspapers (going fast)
- Letters (and the post office!)
- Calculators, calendars, and globes
- Dozens more every year

Many of these industries saw it coming; some fared better than others. Half of travel agents are still here (for now). People are reading more books than ever, but on e-readers. Kodak is bankrupt, even though Kodak *invented* the digital camera.

Think about that light from a dead star, and remember the Golden Innovation Ratio. Seventy percent of your new income will come from those radical ideas you must nurture.

Questions to Kick-Start Innovation

1. When was your organization formed? Was its founding core idea radical?
2. Would your current culture approve it?
3. Do you have any radical idea in work?

Connect Ideas

"Creativity is just connecting things."
—*Steve Jobs*

Connecting the dots is a key attribute of innovators.

The invention of the Swiffer mop came after someone in Procter & Gamble Research put a diaper (they make Pampers) on the end of a mop.

The invention of teeth whitening strips came from combining a thin film, dental cleaning experience, and bleach.[15]

Much of the success of the iPod was the connection to iTunes and the web, which made downloading songs a breeze.

In order to connect, you have to have a wide-ranging knowledge of all the possibilities out there to connect with.

When I first had responsibility for EAASY SABRE, the precursor to Travelocity, I requested our system be hooked up to the Internet, which I'd read about in *Popular Science* magazine. I thought this would be much better than AOL and CompuServe, where we were shackled by their design requirements.

"Sorry," I was told, "the US government owns the Internet. Only educational and nonprofit uses are permitted."

Ten years later, when it became legal to be on the Internet, Travelocity was the result.

I believe that reading widely and attending conferences on fields outside your own is a great way to become more creative. Simply said, *if you want to be innovative, you can't be insular.*

When I took over computer, desktop, and network operations at American, I wanted to push our two thousand employees into the future. They were running an ancient mainframe and network; they needed to know what was happening in the rest of the IT world.

So I got the idea to invite all the IT luminaries I could find to participate in an upcoming employee conference. Knowing they were too busy to drop everything and attend in person, I made them a proposition they couldn't refuse. I would send a film crew to *their* office or film a short interview with them the next time they connected at the Dallas-Fort Worth airport. I made it easy to say yes by promising it would only take ten minutes.

An amazing number accepted. I got senior executives from Microsoft, Sun, IBM, Amdahl, AST, Cisco, and many others to participate. I interviewed them about their best practices, lessons learned, vision for the future, and what they wish someone had told them early in their career.

At one point to prompt some controversy, I asked if we could play some word association. I told them, "I'll say one word. Please give your first-thought response without second-guessing it." The word was SABRE, the name of our system.

Predictably, the IBM exec said, "Reliable, vast in scale."

The Amdahl (another mainframe maker) guy said, "Profitable, scalable, the best airline system." Bill Gates took another view. He said, "Useful, in its time," a not-so-subtle way of saying we were way out of date.

The irrepressible Scott McNealy, CEO of SUN, said, "Hairball." It was exactly the response I wanted and our company needed. *Hairball* was the kick in the pants we needed to hear. As the saying goes, "You're not a prophet in your own land."

Gates and McNealy were the *gods* of IT at that time. If *they* thought our time had passed and we were running a hairball, maybe we were. Having gotten our employees' attention, I could then lay out my vision for our future and our need to innovate quickly.

Listening to others can set you on the path to change. You may not like or agree with their opinion, but their outside perspective may be just what your company needs to see itself as others see it. IT should be bringing new technology to marketing with ideas on how to use IT. Marketing should be introducing ways IT can help them improve. As Roger Iger of Disney says, "If you're not curious about technology and its potential impact on your life, then you have no clue how it's impacting someone else's life."

Questions to Kick-Start Innovation

1. How do you keep from being insular? How do you stay up to date on what's happening in other industries?
2. What's an example of how you listened to an outside perspective or expert to connect ideas in a new way?

IDEA 40

Where Does Innovation Start in a Company?

"The key to success is to get out into the store and listen to what the associates have to say. It's important for everyone to get involved. Our best ideas come from clerks and stockboys."
—Sam Walton

I used to think innovation in an organization started at the top, because the top has all the information, right?

When I was at AA, everyone wrote memos, which were distilled, rewritten, and, if they were good, eventually made their way to our president, Bob Crandall. He consumed mountains of information. He was a very smart guy, and he had access to all the information. As a result, he had some wonderful ideas.

It is also true, however, that many of the best ideas in any company often come from the bottom of the org chart—the front-line employees whose daily job puts them in direct touch with the customers and products.

The good news is that today almost everyone in a company has access to that information, as most companies are quite transparent with their corporate data.

At Travelocity, we initially held employee meetings every few weeks. Back then we could meet in a small room. I'd stand on a desk (really) and update everyone on everything that was going on. I vividly recall standing there the first time we sold a million dollars in a week!

In those meetings, we always asked people to contribute their ideas on what we should work on next. I'm convinced our rapid growth was at least partially due to keeping everyone excited by keeping them in the loop.

That's also where we got the idea, from one of our customer service agents, for paging customers to notify them when their flight was late.

This service was a huge hit with the press and eventually with customers as they got more digital devices.

Another wonderful idea came from one of our airfare programmers. He saw how volatile airfares were and thought, "Why not alert our customers as to the best time to buy?"

Great idea. We set up a program that allowed people to "watch" the airfares to cities where they wanted to travel. Later we refined it to automatically send those customers e-mails when the price dropped, which was magic for our customers.

You've heard of MBWA—Management By Walking Around? I believe in the power of tapping into the brain trust of front-line people, so I started wandering around our offices and just popping into cubes to sit with employees and shoot the breeze.

These conversations let me know what was *really* going on in the company and also generated some leading-edge innovations.

I must say the vice presidents, directors, and managers who were between me and that employee on our org chart didn't always appreciate these visits. Some of them seem to be worried what the employees might say and were afraid they might look bad. My thought about that was, "Well, if you bothered to do this yourselves, you wouldn't have that problem!"

I'm not alone in finding that middle managers don't always welcome MBWA by their leader. John Donahoe of eBay said, "I try to talk to different people at different levels...The people I contact like it, but their bosses and bosses' bosses don't."[16]

Today leaders of companies large and small can "wander around" simply by being part of a company's social network. Products like Yammer and Chatter (both corporate Twitter-like products) allow you to track ideas and jump into the flow of conversations. As Lord Rothmore, chairman of the *Daily Mail*, said, "I've gotten (through Chatter) more employee ideas in three months than in the last twelve years!"[17] That's impressive.

Tom Davenport pointed out in the *Harvard Business Review* that EMC Corporation used a Twitter-like tool to ask employees how to save money and even where to cut employees. Thousands of employees participated, and the cuts were efficient and less painful than if they'd come from the top.[18]

If the best ideas in a company come from your front-line employees, why don't they just flow to the top? As you will learn in the next chapter, it is all about the *Bozone Layer*.

Questions to Kick-Start Innovation

1. Where does innovation start in your organization? Do the majority of creative ideas flow from the top or from your front-line employees?
2. Do you believe in MBWA? How do you keep front-line employees in the loop—and how do you encourage and elicit their ideas for doing things better?

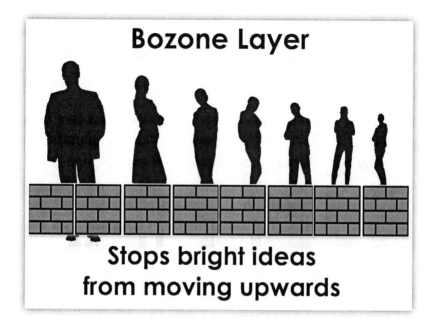

Bozone Layer

Stops bright ideas from moving upwards

Break Through the Bozone Layer

"Innovation that happens from the top down tends to be orderly but dumb. Innovation that happens from the bottom up tends to be chaotic but smart."
—Curtis Carlson, CEO, SRI International

The Bozone Layer?[19]

No, we're not talking about global warming here. The Bozone Layer is that impenetrable layer of middle management that vents great ideas from moving upward.

Even if you have articulated the need for change shown them the burning platform, many midlevel man afraid to recommend disruptions of SOP (standard operating procedures), usually with good reason. They have seen what happens to those who recommend new ideas.

First, they are put in charge of them, doubling their workload with no incentives. Second, if the project fails, they become the fall guy. Or, third, their recommendation is met with initial praise, then disappears into the corporate ether and is never heard from again.

Where's the win in that?

Employees need to be convinced by your actions (see Idea 18: Your Wake Is Larger Than You Imagine) that you genuinely want change. Make it evident through your actions that you don't just *claim* to be OK with experimentation, you go to bat for innovators who dare to contribute "there's a better way" ideas.

Slogans aren't enough. How many times have you seen a vision or mission statement that makes grandiose claims about the company being forward looking and innovative, and it is clear from their products that they simply aren't?

Wandering around talking to people in their cubes, and really listening, will let you know when ideas are stuck. Then you have to make a very loud noise that you won't put up with that behavior.

Reach down and break through!

Questions to Kick-Start Innovation

1. Have you seen the Bozone Layer in your company?
2. If it is there (I'm sure it is), can you go find an idea and trumpet it loudly when you break through?

What Happened to the Lab?

"Internal marketing is more important than external marketing. That's more true today than it's ever been."
—*Tom Stewart, chief marketing officer, Booz & Company*

Wasn't the lab where great ideas used to come from? Thankfully, there are still great labs out there. I recently heard a presentation by the head of the IBM research lab, where they are doing wonderful work with Watson, the computer that won *Jeopardy*.

Guess what Watson is doing these days? He has moved on to diagnosing cancer! Go Watson!

Unfortunately, many great labs, like Bell Labs, are closed. Wall Street rarely lets companies invest enough in long-term research, and many companies have moved the lab into the business, as they've found that the lab must be closer to the business. Google famously lets all its engineers spend 20 percent of their time experimenting; it's a virtual lab.

Moving the lab into the business can help overcome one of innovation's biggest obstacles: winning buy-in to your idea. Too many times, ideas from the lab scientists weren't approved, not because they weren't viable, but because the scientists didn't have the internal marketing clout and connections to get the right people excited about them.

Having a "skunk works" that develops products can sometimes be the answer. The famous Lockheed Skunk Works succeeded wonderfully by taking technologies from Lockheed and advancing them. Of course, since all their projects were *top secret*, who could find out and object!

When I was CIO at SABRE, I had an organization working for me called SABRE Labs. It was a pure R&D function with a substantial budget. The lab came up with some terrific ideas. They thought of the mobile phone boarding pass long before any airline. They showed bookable hotels on a map years before the online agencies did and demonstrated how a consumer could track their lost bag on the Internet.

These were all great ideas. The problem? The business units rejected them all. The value and potential of these ideas was there all the time; our lab team simply lacked the *sales* skills necessary to persuade decision makers to say yes. In fact, some of these ideas were later implemented by competitors and proved profitable.

This isn't unusual; Xerox's PARC Research Center invented the computer mouse, the graphic user interface, the local area network, and many more products *never used by Xerox.*

My favorite rejected product is one I invented (and for which I received a patent) called Goal Oriented Travel Planning. The idea is, you book a meeting in a city on your Outlook calendar, push the travel button, and the system does the rest.

For example, if you're in Dallas and your meeting is in New York at noon on Tuesday, the system knows you have to leave

Monday, need to book a hotel near the meeting site, and, per your profile history, knows you prefer to take a cab from the airport. It geolocates your preferred brand of hotel close to the meeting and recommends your favorite cuisine (Italian) at a nearby restaurant.

The system does all this for you. In moments, you're presented with a few choices of flights, hotels, and car rental options based on your travel profile. We built a working prototype and showed it to our business unit. They were not impressed.

I had enough muscle to arrange for a focus group. The results were positive, but customers wanted to see behind the curtain. They wanted to know how the flight or hotel was selected, what wasn't picked, and what they were "missing out on."

The business unit said, "See...the customers want to do it themselves," and killed the project. That idea died, and it was a high-potential idea, but I didn't market it well enough and didn't get the division to sign up early to pay for its development.

The lesson? Plan the marketing of your idea as carefully as you plan the idea itself.

Questions to Kick-Start Innovation

1. Does your organization have a lab, access to lab, or a "skunk works" that develops products for your company? What role does it play in your innovation efforts?
2. Do your lab scientists have the skills to effectively market and sell their projects to decision makers? If not, are they given training or teamed with sales strategists who do?
3. What's an idea that didn't succeed—and was viable—but the team wasn't able to win buy-in?

Do More with Less

"Put money in thy purse."
—Shakespeare

You might think all this innovation will cost a lot, but you can do more with less today.

As of this writing, I understand that Travelocity has about three thousand employees. Kayak.com has about one hundred and seventy. And yet the two companies have approximately the same number of Internet visitors.

Why the difference? In part, it simply has to do with the time when Travelocity was developed. There were no tools to build Internet companies when we started; we built it with stone tools.

And Travelocity is now over fifteen years old. That is a lot of legacy to support.

But the major differences are because of the huge change the web has made in how companies are built.

At Kayak, we obtained all our customers through search for the first five years. We did *no* brand advertising. That was much more efficient and cost millions less.

We don't have telephone-based customer service (we do answer e-mails), and Google led the way here. Customers don't expect us to provide that level of service.

We aren't a travel agency, so we don't have to issue tickets, collect money, do refunds, and all the hundreds of things that agents do (and take lots of people). We are simply a search company.

Our servers are in the cloud.

Much of our software is open source.

It all adds up to a very efficient, low-cost model.

And it is a model that works for innovation. While it is interesting that Apple and HP started in a garage, it is well to remember that Facebook started in a dorm room!

Between the tools of the web, cheap prototyping tools like 3-D printing, and crowdsourcing, you can test and even implement your idea today without spending huge amounts of capital.

Questions to Kick-Start Innovation

1. How can your organization break away from its traditional processes and really do more with less?
2. Can you find outside services you can use for a fraction of your internal, "transfer-priced" cost, at least for now?
3. Who has to agree to take some risk and "do it on the cheap"?

Install Sensors

"Your most unhappy customers are your greatest source of learning."
—*Bill Gates*

Can you build sensors into your business to understand what your customers want next?

Analyze search terms to identify what people are looking for related to your core products and services. Then identify what *doesn't* show up on your website. If a lot of people want something related to your area of expertise and they *can't* find it on your website, that's a red-flag measure of unmet need.

If your customer wants something you don't have, innovate it. That's a product or service whose time has come.

An analysis of FAQ and support searches will tell you much the same thing. What feature is missing that they are reaching for?

My French brother-in-law owns a company that manufactures sawmill equipment. When I first met him, he was on the phone constantly with customers all over the world, diagnosing problems. More times than not, he'd end up flying an engineer to some remote site to fix a simple problem.

As time went on, he started including a fax machine with every order so the client could send drawings of where the problem was located. Later he added a dial-up modem so he and his clients could remotely diagnose problems.

Today his clients' mills are connected to the Internet. With sensors embedded in every machine, the machine phones home to report maintenance issues and failure analysis. Now his engineers don't have to jump on planes. They stay home, quickly serving their clients. They also improve product performance and innovate the future.

Putting sensors into your product can increase sales too. Progressive insurance puts a monitor in your car for thirty days to analyze your driving habits and offer better pricing. A new Bluetooth-connected toothbrush monitors brushing habits and will certainly sell more toothpaste. Sensors let you learn what customers actually *do* with your product.

Questions to Kick-Start Innovation

1. Are you monitoring search terms to find out what your customers want—and whether you have it? Explain.
2. Do you have sensors installed in your products and sites?
3. How is that improving customer service and satisfaction?

IDEA 45

Turn Customers into Sentries

"Sentries see what's coming before the rest of us."
—Joel Johnson, author

Sentries are on the front line, listening to what's happening. (The photo above is a sentry listening for bombers in World War I.) Sentries are your early warning system if things are going wrong. But how do you put them to work in a business?

At Travelocity I put a British phone booth in the main hall. If you picked up the phone, you could listen in on customer service calls. Every person in the company, from the guy in the mail room to me, had to listen to two customer service calls a month and then have ideas for these two questions at the next staff meeting.

1. How can we improve the company and the product so people don't have to call us?
2. Until we get things fixed, how do we give our customer service agents the best "work-around"—which is a way of saying, "How can they deal with this issue in the interim while we're developing a permanent solution?"

As you can imagine, this proactive system kept our entire team in touch with our customers and kept us focused on how we *could* meet their needs instead of why we *weren't* meeting them.

Kayak.com is a search company. Like Google, we don't take phone calls, but we do get e-mails. Lots of e-mails. Our CTO, Paul English, determined it would be smart to send those e-mails to our programmers instead of creating a customer service department.

Astounding, right? Programmers are expensive. But I guess our slogan is, "Give the pain to the people who cause the pain." Paul's brilliant idea keeps the programmers close to what the customer wants and needs. They have an incentive to fix problems quickly, as they don't want more e-mails, plus they're constantly seeing what new products customers are suggesting, so they stay on top of thinking ahead to what they can build next.

Many companies have "rave" websites where customers are invited to rave (or complain) about their products. Glad Wrap has a site called 1000 Uses and Duck Tape has something similar.

At WD40 (where they have two thousand customer ideas posted), they discovered that Florida customers were using WD40 to remove bugs from their car hoods. Anyone who has lived in Florida in the spring has been through "love bug season" and knows what a pain it is to get them off the car before they ruin the finish. Why was WD40 excited about this idea? Because spraying WD40 on your car uses *lots* of WD40!

Customers will tell you what they are thinking—if you just listen.

Questions to Kick-Start Innovation

1. Do you have a "fun" way to listen in to customer calls? What do you do with that input—that feedback?
2. Do you have a website where customers can rave and complain—thereby giving you a possible "next big thing"? What's a successful innovation you got from it?

Clay in the Customer's Hands

"It is not the strongest of the species that survives, nor the most intelligent that survives. It is the one most responsive to change."
—*Charles Darwin*

One more chapter about the importance of listening to your customers—and understanding that *their* perception of your product is more important than *yours.*

In a way, your products and services are clay in the hands of your customers. They shape your success *if* you listen and adapt.

Someone once said, "Technique follows technology." We simply don't always know where technology will lead us because it's how customers actually *use* the technology that trumps its original, intended purpose.

For example, Alexander Graham Bell thought the telephone would be a tool for the deaf. Edison thought the phonograph would be a dictation machine.

Their initial intent for their inventions was changed and shaped by others into the blockbuster products they eventually became.

Our mobile app at Kayak.com has more than seventeen million downloads, making it currently the most downloaded travel booking application. When it was created, we thought it would be used mostly for last-minute changes, like, "My meeting ran over—what's the closest hotel and the earliest flight out tomorrow?"

We quickly discovered, to our surprise, customers were using it just like their desktop computer. They were booking two weeks out!

So we went back to the drawing board to modify the app to better serve how our customers actually wanted to use it. And lately behavior is changing again!

Comedian George Carlin said, *"What did we go back to before there were drawing boards?"*

If your customers are telling you they like to use your product differently than you'd intended, don't argue with them, and don't tell them they've got it wrong. Head back to the drawing board.

Questions to Kick-Start Innovation

1. What is an example of a product or service your organization created, and your customers shaped it into something that was better suited for their needs?
2. Did you follow their lead and adapt your product and service to be more in alignment with their usage? How so?

Reframe the Problem

"Discovery consists of seeing what everybody has seen
and thinking what nobody has thought."
—*Albert von Szent-Györgyi*

I've talked about my brother, Dewitt, who gives presentations using his dramatic images as metaphors for life's lessons. One of his most popular points is about the power of "reframing."

To demonstrate this, Dewitt shows a photo of a waterfall cascading down a cliff face in Yosemite National Park. The crowd usually oohs and aahs because it is such a beautiful shot.

Then he points out that it's important to use a different lens to look at things from another point of view, and he flashes to the next image.

The audience gasps out loud because Dewitt used a telephoto lens to zoom in, and there, clinging to the cliff face halfway down, is a scraggly little tree growing out of a crack in the rock.

Dewitt points out that we need both a wide-angle lens and a telephoto lens when looking at problems—a wide-angle lens focus to see the big picture, and a telephoto to zoom in to see if there are any details we've overlooked.

Photographers constantly reframe their vision to get the best shot. It is just as important for you as an innovator to reframe your vision if you want the best idea.

Here's an example. At Travelocity we wanted to provide graphic seat maps so customers could see available seats on their upcoming flight and click on the seat they wanted. That's the norm today, but when we thought this up, no one had done it.

SABRE already had seat maps, but given their nongraphic capability, those maps were simply a series of Xs and Os, and to book, you had to type in the seat number you desired (32B).

Our challenge was how to obtain the graphic maps we thought we needed. Most airlines had them published in their flight magazines, but to collect the literally thousands of configurations seemed a gargantuan task. We were at an impasse, so we brought one of our best programmers into our brainstorming group. He immediately said, "Why don't we just take the SABRE map, parse it, and light up a graphic with the available seats? We won't know where the kitchens or lavs are, but it'll be good enough."

It sure was. We were looking with the wrong lens. He reframed the discussion and produced a workable solution in minutes.

Next time you're at an impasse, step back and look at the situation with a new lens. Ask someone outside the group to contribute a different point of view. Imagine you're holding a camera in your hands and reframe the issue—zoom in and study the details. Step back and look at the big picture. Aaahh, there you are—the right answer just came into focus.

Questions to Kick-Start Innovation

1. Are you stuck? Imagine you're holding a camera. Look at the situation with a different lens. What do you see?
2. When were you at an impasse and someone with an outside perspective reframed the discussion and problem?

Walk in Their Shoes

"To understand the man you must first walk a mile in his moccasins."
—Indian proverb

Many companies are convinced customers want *more, more, more.*

I don't agree. Customers today are driven by speed and convenience. Great design is usually very simple, but it can be very difficult to achieve.

Apple simplified using computers with the graphic user interface on the Mac. Then they simplified using an MP3 player with the iPod. As a result of these simplifications, their products are hailed as the best, both aesthetically and functionally.

As someone who travels frequently for business, I'm a premiere member with many hotel brands. I often get upgraded to a suite, and there is almost always a bowl of fruit in the room with a nice note from the general manager thanking me for staying.

But in all the thousands of hotels I've visited, I've never received a card saying, "I'm having a small cocktail party tonight with our premiere members who are staying with us. I hope you'll join us at 6:30 p.m. as my guest for complimentary refreshments. I would enjoy meeting you and hearing about your experience with, and your recommendations for, our hotel."

Why not? It wouldn't be inconvenient, as many GMs of top hotels *live* in the hotel. Plus, they would be honoring their frequent users and finding out firsthand what they like, don't like, what keeps them coming back, and what chases them away. Talk about crowdsourcing!

I recently stayed at a four-star hotel. I've stayed there more than twenty-five times in the past few years. My meetings were not until the evening, so, having arrived early, I had an entire day to sit in the wonderful easy chair in my room and work on a new speech.

Except when I arrived, there was no easy chair in the room. In its place was a chaise lounge. Now, I don't know about you, but the only good use I've seen for a chaise lounge was in Goya's painting *The Naked Maja*! I called the front desk and said, "Could you please move me to a room with an easy chair?"

"Oh, we don't have those anymore," came the reply. "All our rooms now have a chaise lounge!"

I simply refuse to believe executives talked to a single customer before making that change. Do you know any road warriors who "lounge" while on the road?

The same thinking (or lack of it) must have gone into placing the very warm down duvets in my Miami hotel, where it was 100 degrees. Or adding computerized controls to my shower in LA that rivaled MS-DOS in complexity.

My favorite example is when—try as I might—I was unable to open the soap provided in the shower. I wrote the GM (enclosing the unopened soap): "Sir, Imagine you are naked and wet. You have no sharp objects, as the TSA took them all away. Now, you try and open this soap!"

I received a polite note back. "Dear Mr. Jones, Thank you very much for your letter. *We have changed our soap!*"

Good for that GM for taking action on my complaint, but why did it take me to point that out? I'm willing to wager that whoever bought the soap never tried it in "field conditions."

From now on, keep your antenna up for "duh" features that could make products more user-friendly. Why don't hotels have curtains that close, plugs near the bed, lights you can read by, and showers with handles that make sense? It's because business leaders don't use their own products before foisting them off on customers. If they did, they'd innovate and keep customers happy and coming back.

Questions to Kick-Start Innovation

1. Have you been in a situation where you thought, "*Why* do they do this? It makes no sense!" What was that?
2. Do you know who your 20 percent is? How do you focus on and honor your premiere customers so they remain happy and keep coming back?

Look Beyond What Is Immediately Apparent

*"A lot of times people don't know what they want
until you show it to them."*
—*Steve Jobs*

Market research is great.

Customer feedback and employee input are great.

But sometimes you just have to look beyond what's right in front of you and take a leap of faith to pursue your vision.

Once I went with some other managers to present the concept of e-ticketing to the executive committee at American Airlines. We explained that with this new idea, we wouldn't have to print tickets, sort them, count them, and ship them back to accounting. It would save lots of money.

The committee listened to our case and immediately took exception to what we felt was a visionary innovation:

—"What would our customers do for receipts?"
—"They like paper tickets!"
—"Leave us, go from this room!"

AA, the leader in so many things, was a latecomer to e-tickets because those particular decision makers focused on the objections instead of the potential.

Another time, we proposed adding power to each bank of seats on our planes so passengers could plug in their laptops. Every time I'd fly, I'd see seatmates sigh and shut down their computers, frustrated because their batteries had died and they couldn't finish their projects. It was a very expensive proposal, and the AA leaders simply couldn't see the need. Then I realized, *none* of them had a laptop (except the head of IT). They were all still having their secretaries type memos, and none of them were doing e-mail. Laptops were not part of their world, so they didn't see the problem or the need.

Kayak.com was a result of looking beyond the apparent. We observed that hundreds of thousands of people would search Travelocity, Orbitz, and Expedia and then leave to purchase their tickets directly from the airlines. We looked ahead and envisioned a product where people could search everything they want and then click and purchase directly from the supplier.

So look beyond the apparent. What can you envision that doesn't yet exist—and that could give customers more of what they want and need?

Questions to Kick-Start Innovation

1. What's an example of a visionary product that could make life easier, more efficient, or more enjoyable for your customers?
2. Look beyond the apparent. What is a service that doesn't yet exist but would be a first-of-its-kind innovation that would add value for customers and contribute to your company's bottom line?

Leverage Social Media

"Activate your fans, don't just collect them like baseball cards."
—Jay Baer, Convince & Convert

Kudos to Jay Baer for that great advice.

I often hear entrepreneurs talk about how many friends their company has on Facebook, how many followers they have on Twitter.

I want to ask them, "Are you using them for innovation?"

Beau Ties, a bow-tie company in Vermont, recently disclosed to *Internet Retailer* that they have been tapping into their customer base to design their product line.

The CEO explained that it takes about six months from the time they design a tie until it arrives at their warehouse for shipment to customers. So in July they put their proposed Christmas tie designs on Facebook and let their customers vote on which they should manufacture. That makes a lot more sense than hoping their company buyer can predict what customers might like.

Research shows that customers who "friend" you want just two things: access to deals and to be the first to hear about new products. So treat them like friends, and they will tell their friends.

Susan Abbott of Customer Crossroads posted in her blog, "I was making some dip when I realized for the one hundredth time that when you open the package, you rip the instructions, rendering them unreadable." If that was on your Facebook page, what would you do?

I toured the production line at Cessna Aircraft a while back. As I went from one assembly station to another, I noticed papers tacked to the pillars. I walked closer and saw they were customer comments. Some genius had taken the time to collect customer feedback forms and post them where every line worker could see them. "I love the workmanship of the seat covers" or "The door insulation leaked and created a loud whistle."

Too often feedback forms are read, filed, and then never seen again. Kudos to Cessna for keeping customer compliments and criticism in sight and in mind...so they stay top of mind.

Questions to Kick-Start Innovation

1. Do you have a system for monitoring Facebook, Twitter, and LinkedIn for innovation?
2. How do you interact with your online tribe and recruit their feedback? How do you make sure employees are updated with social media input so they can act on it?

IDEA 51

Innovation of Crowds

"No one is as smart as all of us."
—*Japanese proverb*

Calling all experts.

Eli Lilly and Procter & Gamble are early examples of the power of using outside resources for innovation.[20]

Lilly's Open Innovation Drug Discovery program lets researchers submit compounds for automated analysis on a Lilly website. They can digitally encode their work to protect their intellectual property, and Lilly can analyze the compound to see if it's worth further testing. Over the last few years, it has analyzed over four hundred submissions and signed several contracts.[21]

P&G found more than 1.5 million scientists worldwide who matched the profile of their own two hundred researchers. They tapped into the power of "outside experts" to produce an amazing multiplier effect.

In a few short (and difficult) years after beginning their "connect and develop" strategy, they increased their externally collaborated development from 15 percent to 35 percent. In addition, more than 45 percent of their new products had elements sourced externally.

P&G also used "technology entrepreneurs" (from their own staff) to collaborate with university professors to mine literature and to keep their eyes open around the world for new ideas.

One such entrepreneur discovered a product in Japan that was eventually modified to become P&G's super-successful Mr. Clean Magic Eraser—a product I use all the time!

External companies have allowed P&G to find ways to print designs on potato chips and add wrinkle fighters to skin creams. I know, I know, potato chip designs may not be your top priority, but they're contributing millions to P&G's bottom line.

In addition to university professors and tech entrepreneurs, open innovators find new collaborations with suppliers, retirees, and laymen who submit ideas over the web.

When seeking outside expert help, it's advantageous to make *broad* statements when defining the direction of the requested investigation. For example, "We need more cleaners that work in cold water for the developing world."

That may sound contrarian; it's just that you want to give open experts the *goal* and let them come up with the *process*. In this case, the less information you give them, the better.

Questions to Kick-Start Innovation

1. Has your company solicited outside experts to aid in your innovation efforts? Who have they brought in? University professors? Retirees? Techies?
2. When seeking outside experts, how did you describe your project goals? Did you find the less you said about the process, the better? Explain.

Innovation of Your Own Crowd

*"Crowdsourcing is the process by which the power of the
many can be leveraged to accomplish feats that
were once the province of a specialized few."*
—*Jeff Howe*

I needed a new logo for my consulting business, and I dreaded
getting this job done.

I've had logos designed for many companies in my career. The
process is often painful, with lots of back-and-forth dialogue with
an ad agency that charges you a fortune and gives you four noth-
ing-special options four months later.

So I decided to do it differently this time.

I searched the web and found several companies, from Mycroburst to 99 Designs, that crowdsource logo design. The company I selected gave me fifty designs from designers all over the world for $200! The winning design was just what I wanted, and the process took days instead of months.

I had a similar experience when my wife inadvertently ripped the side mirror off my car. While trying to put the new one in place, I just couldn't find the last bolt that needed to be removed to get the door panel off.

I went online and found a website called *Just Answers*. Ten minutes and ten dollars (!) later, I had just the answer I needed from a certified Nissan technician and *Just Answers* consultant who was working from home on a weekend.

Curious, I did a little research into *Just Answers* and discovered it was started by a serial entrepreneur in Silicon Valley who was frustrated by not being able to find straight answers to what he thought were simple questions. So he aggregated an online network of experts who reply via e-mail and solve problems.

You can ask a lawyer, doctor, vet, or mechanic just about anything and find out what you need to know…in minutes. They stream sample questions on their home page and include everything from "How do I get a liquor license for my tavern?" to "My father-in-law is traveling and lost all forms of ID…"

Salesforce.com's Chatter is helping many companies toss questions out to their internal experts (and experts they might not even know they have) to quickly find answers to dilemmas.

You already have experts such as these in your company. The trick is to deploy the software so you can use them to innovate in ways you never imagined. Turn your experts into innovators!

Questions to Kick-Start Innovation

1. How can you crowdsource in your own company?
2. Do you have tools in place (Chatter? Yammer?) that could be used as lubricants for innovation?

A	Yes	☐
B	Yes	☐
C	Yes	☐
D	Yes	☐

There Is More Than One Right Answer

"When you can do a common thing in an uncommon way,
you will command the attention of the world."
—George Washington Carver

One more story about my brother, Dewitt, who really is a master at using the creative arts to draw analogies between life and business.

In his talks he makes the point that "there is more than one right answer." He illustrates that idea through photos of the same object from very different views. All right answers, just some are much better than others.

Sakichi Toyoda perfected the process at Toyota Motors of asking "Why?" five times. He believed it took that many questions to get at the heart of why something was done in a certain way.

I agree that going a question deeper is important. Sometimes people give pat answers when asked a question. If they're asked "Why?" again, again, and then again…they have to dig deep to identify the true rationale behind a behavior or belief.

They may discover they're doing something simply because this was how they were taught to do it by their boss twenty years ago or because the manual says so. Well, none of those reasons may be valid in today's rapidly changing circumstances.

I ran across a perfect example of this recently. I imagine many of you have seen the rotating security cameras that have a ball lens that constantly revolves to scan an area.

The problem is the camera eye may be looking left when the bad guy is on the right. In fact, crooks often time the eye to make sure they make their mad dash when it is looking the opposite direction.

So an inventor created another right answer. He took five cell phone cameras, mounted them together, and created a 180-degree mosaic of all the cameras through software. This flat camera provides a more comprehensive image at a fraction of the cost.

Can you imagine what the managers of the camera housing and camera motor department thought of this idea? I suspect it took a very determined innovator (and a leader giving air support) to persevere and get this approved when faced with the objections of those who produced the current product and were invested in the years of infrastructure wrapped around it. Imagine the conversation in the innovation session:

"Why do we use a motor?"
"To rotate the camera."

"Why do we rotate the cameras?"
"To video the entire room."

"Why do we video the entire room?"
"So we don't miss a bad guy."

"Why can't we use many cameras pointed in different directions?"
"Because it would be too expensive to buy that many cameras."

"Why can't we use cell phone cameras and combine them into one unit?"
"Ohhhh."

Remember what it says on the multiple-answer test: "Check all boxes that apply." There is more than one right answer…look for them.

Questions to Kick-Start Innovation

1. Are you a photographer? Have you ever taken many wonderful photos at a gathering or event—and experienced for a fact there's more than one right answer?
2. What's an example at work where, instead of narrowing it down to one option, your team realized you could run with several options because they were all viable? Describe the situation and what happened.

Trading Places

"Are you doing what you're doing today because it works,
or because it was what you were doing yesterday?"
—Dr. Phil McGraw

Sometimes sitting in someone else's chair is what's needed to stir up the innovation soup.

At ADS (a small mini-computer division of American I worked for), the sales and service leaders were constantly carping about each other's departments. Each had great ideas for the other guy's sandbox (and not so many for his own).

The boss got fed up and one day announced, "Jim—as of today you are head of service. John—you are head of sales!"

They were shocked. I thought it was a crazy idea, but they were both talented execs, and in a short time they made many improvements. Getting a new job means you can look under rocks and ask, "Why do we do it this way?"

Remember, ask "Why?" five times. You will be surprised (shocked?) at how many people have no idea why they're doing what they're doing. "I'm just doing what I was told to do." That means people are on automatic pilot, and it's not smart to run a business on automatic pilot with people acting like automatons.

You don't have too long until those stupid processes and products are your own, and the natural style is to start defending them, so move quickly and ask dumb questions.

At Travelocity, I did much the same thing with our customer relationship management system (CRM). The head of marketing was constantly complaining about delays and bad analysis with our CRM system. I got fed up and put him in charge of the system and gave him control of the programmers and data analysts.

I also told him he'd also have to learn to serve the rest of the company, as he was *not* the only customer of CRM. It worked. He shortened feedback loops, decreased time to market, and increased experimentation, which increased overall effectiveness.

Do you have a complainer? Could you put them in charge? It's amazing how being responsible for a process or system transforms you from griping about it to fixing it.

Google and Procter & Gamble tried an "executive exchange" of a few dozen employees for several weeks. They reasoned that P&G (a huge advertiser) and Google (a huge ad network) could learn from each other's perspectives. They were right. Several new products and processes resulted from the swap—and executives came back with renewed appreciation for their current positions.

The CTOs at Kayak and HubSpot recently traded jobs for a day. Afterward, HubSpot CTO Dharmesh Shah said, "The coolest part of the thing (for me) was getting to spend time talking to really smart people that are in a different industry. And I got to ask really simple questions."

One day at American, my boss and mentor (Max Hopper) called me in and said, "I'm moving you to run a team of five hundred programmers!" Shocked, I protested, "But I've never managed programmers. I don't know anything about that."

He told me, "You'll do fine." In fact, it was a wonderful two years, looking under rocks and improving systems. Then I was called in again. This time by Kathy, my new boss, who said, "We're putting you in charge of computer operations, networks, and desktops. It's two thousand people and a budget of $300 million."

"But..." I began. The reply: "Oh, you'll be fine; go get started." Again, moving to a new area allowed me to learn so much and see the company from a broader view. Moving, trading places, taking on new positions stretches us and often stretches our departments and projects.

Southwest Airlines is famous for its very short airplane turn times. This was originally driven because they simply could not afford as many planes as they needed to serve their routes. By cutting turn times, they "created" more planes. Over time they have become so good at this, they could not figure out how to get better. There were no airlines that they could learn from, so they improved by watching Indianapolis 500 pit crews!

Sitting in someone else's chair can be a much better view for innovation.

Questions to Kick-Start Innovation

1. Have you ever had an executive exchange with another company? What benefits emerged from that?
2. Could you create an executive exchange within your organization? What types of different perspectives might it yield if department heads traded places?

Can You Say…Incentives?

"Only in our dreams are we free. The rest of the time we need wages."
—*Terry Pratchett*

Leaders often debate whether it's advantageous to offer incentives for ideas from employees.

Some argue it's part of the job, and people do it willingly and voluntarily because it feels good to contribute and it's tangible proof they're making a difference.

Others believe if employees come up with ideas that save or make a company millions, they deserve to get a piece of that pie.

What do you think? I don't believe it's an either/or situation; I think it's *both*. I think we need ideas and income, dreams and wages.

As Yogi Berra said, "When you come to a fork in the road, take it."

At American Airlines, we had an idea program where employees were paid for ideas based either on the revenue created or expenses that were actually taken out of budget as a result (as determined by a management committee). As in an incentive program, the employees selected gifts from a catalog. I can testify that incentives work, as my wife got a mink coat out of her idea! And I approved hundreds of thousands of dollars in gifts from ideas that saved us millions.

DuPont pays successful teams incentives from $50K to $100K.

One benefit of an incentive program is that it counteracts the attitude that "Around here, if ideas fail, people get fired. If they succeed, they might get a very small raise."

It is true though that for those with innovating in their blood, just getting to push the creative envelope is a significant incentive.

In Tracy Kidder's book *Soul of a New Machine*, he says about a group of veteran developers, "They believed in the rule of pinball: if you win you get to play again." The satisfaction lies in getting to do it again.[22]

Questions to Kick-Start Innovation

1. Does your company offer some type of incentive for contributing cost-saving or revenue-producing ideas? If not, why not? If so, how does that work?
2. Do you believe it is beneficial to offer incentives? Why or why not?
3. What's an example of an employee who contributed an idea that had a major impact on your organization? How was he or she acknowledged or rewarded?

SECTION 5:

Select the Best Ideas

"Have I pushed the creative envelope as much as I've wanted? No, that's why I'm still hungry."
—*Stephen Spielberg*

How Do You Pick the Best Ideas?

"I see the better things, and approve."
—Ovid, 43 BC

Are you old enough to remember (wait for it)...suggestion boxes?

Yes, in decades past, many companies actually used to have a wooden *box* attached to a wall where employees were invited to submit suggestions written on slips of paper.

This system worked sometimes. More often than not, someone's brainchild was slipped into the box and never heard from again.

One of the best ways to pick the best ideas is to make sure ideas are seen by *lots* of people. If an idea's future is in the hands of someone who doesn't want to make waves or someone who delights in playing devil's advocate, that idea may die a quick death and never see the light of day.

When I was working at American Airlines, we had an idea program called IdeAAs in Action (everything at American has two As). The program was adapted from a similar program at GE. Employees would submit ideas to their managers, and if the idea was implemented, they could win valuable prizes based on the economic value of the idea.

It sounds common enough, but there was a crucial difference in this idea program. Ideas were vetted not only by the manager of the department where it was submitted, but *also by two managers of other departments.* This was to get around the default "That would never work here!" syndrome that results from being locked into a status quo they're invested to protect.

Here's an example of how it worked. Before the new program, a mechanic in our maintenance department noted that his friends complained that when they flew on our new regional jets, they didn't get to use a jet bridge into the terminal and had to walk outside in the rain and the snow.

Knowing that these jets were going to be a big part of American's future, he designed a "walk the plank" connecting device, similar to the one on pirate ships, to connect the existing jet bridges designed for the big 747s to the smaller regional jets.

His boss rejected the idea. His logic was that jet bridges were really expensive, and customers only had to walk outside on the stairs for a moment, so it wasn't that big of a deal.

When we put our new IdeAAs in Action program in place, the mechanic resubmitted his idea. This time it was reviewed not only by his own maintenance department, but also by the marketing and operations departments.

This time, it was approved! The operations department knew that if customers had a favorable experience flying our regional jets, they could deploy more of them and lower our costs because we'd be running full airplanes instead of flying half empty.

Marketing loved it because it gave them something new to advertise. Even our legal department chimed in to praise the idea, noting they would have fewer complaints (and lawsuits) from customers who had slipped or fallen as they trudged across the tarmac or carried their bag up the slippery steps in a storm.

As our policy of vetting new ideas through multiple departments grew, I witnessed its many benefits. That prize I mentioned earlier that my wife won? It was a suggestion to make our employee directory available *online.* The same idea that won her a prize had been submitted before, but it had been rejected by the manager of the department who printed the *paper* directories. (Gee...isn't that surprising!)

Want the best ideas to make it through the gauntlet? Make sure they get a wide review.

Questions to Kick-Start Innovation

1. Do you have a version of a suggestion box? What is your program for offering incentives?
2. Do you have a policy in which different departments vet ideas? How has that worked for you?

Reduce Risk with Prototypes

"All models are wrong, but some are useful."
—George Box

Almost every organization has a development budget, something reserved for building new products, but *which* new products?

Over the years, I've seen a bias against the "little" products that, at first look, don't appear as if they'll contribute significantly to the bottom line.

At Travelocity, many of us had come from a very large company. As we grew, we developed the traditional corporate project list. We'd have long meetings where we wrangled over project priorities that moved up or down our have-to-do list, depending on their contribution to revenue, improvement of customer service, fixing infrastructure, etc.

The problem was that we never seemed to be able to get to the exciting stuff, the fun stuff, the stuff we thought customers wanted.

It was hard to prove the revenue contribution of these smaller ideas. The larger projects crowded out the smaller projects.

In addition, since the president (me) was an innovator, I kept coming up with ideas that circumvented the process, and the team wasn't happy about that.

So we did two things.

First, we created a Quick Hits group that worked on any good idea that took under six weeks to deliver.

This solved a problem I used to have at AA. My boss there was convinced that big projects had more value than small ones. I didn't (and don't) believe this was necessarily true. Customers don't care how much effort or time you put into a new feature; they only care what it does for them.

Creating this Quick Hits team allowed us to get a steady flow of new features into the customers' hands. I'm convinced that a continuous pipeline of improvements is a beautiful thing that pays off for all involved in, and around, a company.

In addition, I hired two programmers to work directly for me. Their sole responsibility was to take my ideas and build prototypes quickly that we could then test on the website. As covered in our previous section, you can get almost instant feedback on your ideas online, and that we received!

In addition to creating the prototype of flight paging, this team put airfares on a map, so you could enter how much money you had and we'd tell you where you could afford to go.

We'd put our prototype up and watch what happened. In some cases, like flight paging, the idea was an instant hit, and we started the "official" development process to work out all the service and software issues and ensure it was a quality product (as the prototypes were invariably buggy).

In other cases, customers didn't like the product, but the press loved it (like airfares on a map), so we'd keep it up as a prototype and leverage the PR until the press lost interest and we had another idea to announce.

The payoff was that we at least got to explore our small, short-term Quick Hits ideas, instead of putting them off for the never-gonna-happen "someday" when we weren't so busy and they floated to the top of our to-do list.

Sometimes they succeeded, sometimes not. For example, we built the capability for you to plan a trip with a friend where you were both online at the same time so you could instantly compare schedules and flight preferences...and no one cared!

For every prototype we built that went nowhere, we hadn't invested much; for those that were a success, we could quickly turn them into products.

Questions to Kick-Start Innovation

1. Do you have a committee or team that gives short-term, smaller projects their due? Describe that process.
2. What's an example of a "little" idea that turned out to have a huge return on investment...but might never have been approved if it had to fight its way to the top of the to-do list?

SECTION 6:

Increasing Innovation in a Large Corporation

"Change is hard because people overestimate the value of what they have—and underestimate the value of what they may gain by giving that up."
—*Belasco and Stayer,* Flight of the Buffalo

Don't Let Your Delivery Muscle Outweigh Your Discovery Muscle

"In so many large companies, they let their 'delivery muscle'—in effect, how they get work done—completely outweigh the 'discovery muscle' of trying to innovate and find new ways of doing things."
—Ronald Shaich, CEO, Panera Bread

Innovation in a large company is much different than innovation in a small one.

Having worked in large publically traded companies (American Airlines, EarthLink, La Quinta), small companies (Vega Travel, AgencyDataSystems, Luxury Link, Smart Destinations), and small ones that grew large (Travelocity, Overture, Kayak.com), I've viewed the differences firsthand.

Travelocity grew up in the SABRE division of the multibillion-dollar American Airlines. American was a great company, with worldwide offices and highly centralized control. Airlines are almost military in their organization and logistical efficiency. SABRE wasn't much different. At the time Travelocity was born, SABRE had sales over a billion and utilized many of the highly centralized services of AA.

There are good things about starting a new idea or project inside a big company:

- You don't need venture capitalists (VCs) or their money.
- You can draw on a large pool of skilled employees.
- It's easy to get offices, computers, phones, etc.
- Their big name can open doors.

There are also difficulties in a big company:

- You don't get the knowledge provided by VCs.
- You don't get the VC network of great start-up people.
- Corporate money comes at a high price:
  o A stunning number of rules;
  o Numbing bureaucracy.

Your new idea will require start-up money and a start-up mentality, but it will be a drag on earnings and will challenge the status quo.

I have four basic prescriptions, covered in the next four chapters, that can help you succeed in leading innovation in a large company. The prescriptions are to build a LOFT:

- Location
- Organization
- Funding
- Team

Questions to Kick-Start Innovation

1. What is your history as a leader? Have you always worked for large corporations? Any experience in small business or start-ups? How has this impacted your ability to initiate innovation and oversee innovation?

L = Location

"Think outside the building."
—*Rosabeth Moss Kantor*

As Travelocity grew, I began looking around for space. I was anxious to both get us out of the AA headquarters and to put us all together. It had been easy for other divisions to resist co-locating their people with us when we didn't have enough space.

Finally, I discovered an unused AA space a few blocks from HQ. It had been the corporate media center, where they made marketing slide shows and videos, and it had been abandoned in a cutback. It was broken up in strange ways, had darkrooms, editing bays, and an amazing viewing room with room for thirty people with a massive movie screen. It smelled of chemicals and was dirty and stained, but it was ours for the taking.

The change in the team when we got together was amazing. We built our own culture. At the time AA still required you to wear a suit and tie. We quickly ditched that idea, opting for the more casual clothes that were better suited (hah) for our surroundings and our ten-plus hour days. AA had very high-quality furniture; we had junk…no one cared.

Because we were hard to find, I ordered a sign for the building with the Travelocity logo. I immediately got a call from facilities saying that such a sign was not allowed. No other division or department had an external sign; we were all just "AA." We were told to take it down. Somehow, that directive got "lost."

A few weeks later, two facilities workmen came and carted the sign away.

Our team got our revenge. A month later, funds were approved to repave our parking lot. Gazing outside at the wet cement, I thought of a way we could permanently claim our space. I asked one of our design artists to go out and "play in the mud." Moments later, our logo had been etched into the wet cement. Rule makers didn't see it until it was too late. It's still there.

So one way to successfully lead innovation inside a large company is to think outside the building. Move out, or at least move together in a concentrated space within your structure so your *location* can help you create a distinctive culture.

By the way, Steve Jobs subscribed to this notion. He moved the Mac division out of Apple HQ, noting, "It's better to be a pirate than join the navy."

Questions to Kick-Start Innovation

1. Do you have a separate location for your innovative project? Is it off-site or outside the building? Where?
2. How does having your own space help you build your own culture? How does that support innovative projects?

O = Organizational Structure

"If you had to identify, in one word, the reason why the
human race has not achieved, and never will achieve,
its full potential, that word would be 'meetings.'"
—Dave Barry, Pulitzer Prize–winning humorist

If you've ever sat through one of those interminable meetings where nothing gets done, for hours at a time, you probably agree with Dave.

And the word "committees" can be substituted for "meetings."

The first instinct of many managers when confronted with how to proceed with a new idea is to create a *committee* composed of affected departments to push the idea forward. That can work.

But remember, corporations are organized in divisions, and "divide" is sometimes the operative word here.

Employees retain strong loyalty to their departments: ops to ops, marketing to marketing, and so on. Their incentives are often based on how their division performs, not on the success of this new venture, and sometimes those two priorities are at odds.

One way to avoid conflicts of interests is to create a separate organizational structure around a big idea. We did that around Internet commerce, as did Best Buy, REI, and many others.

Travelocity began as part of the product development organization. It was a team focused on *product* design and *business* design. We had to go to other divisions for promotion, accounting, programming, legal, etc.

Eventually we knew we had to bring many of these functions into the team to be able to move at speed and focus on the product.

With a separate organization, you have the opportunity to build a team culture that is centered on, and committed to, the success of *their* idea. This isn't easy!

At Travelocity, once we formed our new organizational structure and brought everyone into the same space, some divisional leaders insisted their employees still (at least on paper) report to them. Those staff members were required to attend weekly staff meetings of their respective areas. And their incentives and salary were determined by their original division, so we lost a very potent carrot for success.

Over time we persuaded the divisional leaders to drop the staff-meeting requirement (partly a spy function) and suggested we write *joint* performance reviews. We eventually were able to relocate these staff into the same office with us. Only then did we really begin to build a team culture.

We didn't bring all departments into Travelocity until we became a public company. In the meantime we had to use other departments, which created an obstacle course that was only surmounted by a determined leader providing "air cover."

Travelocity reported to the CEO of SABRE. She (and later he) provided valuable clout in support of the idea. That was critically important. The other departments wanted our money, as they were certain (and were probably right) that they could provide an instant return while we were losing big bucks. But our CEOs focused on the long term and were eventually proven right when we spun out of SABRE for $2 *billion.*

The infighting between departmental priorities became so heated at one point, the CEO decided to hold a debate to see whether we should keep or sell Travelocity.

I was not allowed to participate. Employees from Travelocity and the other divisions argued on both sides. All the senior team from SABRE was present. Perhaps the CEO knew in advance how it would turn out; he never told me. I waited, sweating, for the results. We prevailed, at least partially because our organizational structure had given us the autonomy to prove our potential. Winning also pretty much stopped the carping and infighting.

Questions to Kick-Start Innovation

1. Do you have a separate organizational structure for a big idea that's being implemented? What is that?
2. Has this new division encountered resistance from other departments? How have those conflicts or competing priorities been dealt with?

F = Funding

"Wealth is not about having a lot of money;
it's about having lots of options."
—*Chris Rock*

Any business hates losing money. Public companies most of all.

If an idea has been around awhile but is not performing as well as hoped, if it, at one time, made money, management will probably continue to pour money into it. They have a lot at stake.

But when an idea is unproven and has never made money for the company, it is hard to stay the course when there's no guarantee of an ROI.

Venture capitalists are used to this, of course. They know the majority of their start-ups won't make it. They expect new ventures to consume lots of cash before they go positive, and they're prepared for it.

Big companies just aren't built that way.

Leaders of innovations in large corporations have to have the courage of their convictions. And they need to have the clout and determination to fend off the other department heads who are contending they would use this money more effectively and produce a more immediate ROI.

At Travelocity, our budget was held at the SABRE CEO level. For a long time only the CEO could see how much we were costing the company. That proved to be crucial, as it silenced the critics, who didn't have the necessary financial ammo to take us down because they didn't have access to the actual numbers.

Many companies use this hub-and-spoke type of innovation budgeting, with the center holding the R&D dollars so individual departments don't have the visibility to cause trouble.

If you have the option to have a "black" budget, like the CIA, it can make things easier because it allows you to operate under the radar in the early stages when your venture is all expenditure, no income.

Questions to Kick-Start Innovation

1. What is an innovation project you're working on? How is it being funded?
2. Are you getting grief from other departments who are convinced they could be putting your budget to better use? How are you dealing with that?
3. What is a proactive option you could use to create a financing structure that protects your numbers?

T = Team

"Hiring is like putting together an orchestra."
—*Susan Credle, chief creative officer Leo Burnett*

In section 2 we addressed the importance of building the right team. We talked about hiring a diverse mix of people: experienced people and inexperienced, older and younger, people not like you.

Sometimes that is easier said than done…especially in a large organization as opposed to a start-up. Start-ups often have an unfair advantage in hiring; they can offer stock options, relaxed cultures, and the excitement of a big idea.

Corporations usually have to hire from within and have a tough time removing nonperformers. However, corporations do offer great benefits, stability, decent starting salaries, and chances for upward mobility.

I encourage internal start-ups to hire from the outside *and* the inside. As discussed, you need external experts to provide the diversity that pushes everyone to think different. Debate is healthy. If everyone has the same background, debate is lackluster, which means ideas aren't being rigorously challenged, a prerequisite for looking at all sides of the beach ball.

Don't hire all outsiders, though.

Once at SABRE I managed a group of one hundred SABRE programmers building a software system for the new French high-speed trains in a joint venture with the French railroad. The group worked in new organizational structures, partnered with a very different culture, and worked in Paris. They were even housed in portable trailers, cold in winter, hot in summer, with everyone crammed together. However, being in close proximity was great for innovation, as we fed off each other's energy.

We had to teach an airline reservation system all about trains. But the core of our work was based on the SABRE system we knew inside out, and that knowledge combined with the French knowledge of railroad systems made it work. It was a grand success and is one of my favorite examples of how combining the strengths of two teams can scale results in record time.

Later the company won another large software project that was also travel related. This time, for some reason, they decided to hire almost *all* new people, program in a new language, use new product management systems, and design totally new systems from the ground up around an idea that had never been tried!

It failed miserably. They didn't build on the strengths the company had to innovate further.

Questions to Kick-Start Innovation

1. Think about the demographics of your team. Is it a diverse mix?
2. How have you leveraged the different perspectives to expedite innovation in your company?

Managing the Angry Crowd

"It may have escaped your notice, but life isn't fair."
—*Severus Snape*

I've talked before about how much "air cover" the leader has to provide to ensure the success of new ideas. The changes brought about by a new venture will upset the status quo, and rules will be broken. Participants in the new venture may reap great rewards, and perhaps the old guard won't.

For most of the period of its growth, leaders who understood the concept of air cover protected Travelocity. At a critical point, however, that air cover was withdrawn.

Even though Travelocity became a public company, we were still 70 percent owned by SABRE. As we grew and the future of travel agents became more uncertain, SABRE decided that they needed to buy Travelocity back so they could determine its direction (something they could not do while it was a public company).

One day I got a note from my chairman that said, "Form a special committee of independent directors. We are going to take you private." It was a long and difficult process, but we got it done.

As the time to close the deal approached, I called the chairman and said, "I need your help. The way the executive employment contracts are written, the leaders have to leave the company if they want to get paid for their stock options. These options are big money to them, and I believe they all will quit to get paid. We should find a way around this clause."

"Well, I just don't think we can do that," he retorted. "It would not be fair to those executives at SABRE who won't get such a payout."

I was incredulous. "Hang on a minute. If you do this, you will have just paid $500 million to buy back the company and not have the executives in place to run it!"

He replied that he thought they could handle it with promotions and transfers, and that my plan "just would not be fair to the SABRE guys." I pointed out that "the SABRE guys" had not created $2 billion in value, but to no avail!

Although he said I could stay, almost *all* of us left. At this critical juncture, Travelocity got entirely new management and, frankly, hit quite a speed bump in growth.

The lesson here is that life isn't fair. Change will break some eggs, and as a leader you have to manage the angry crowd who didn't innovate, and perhaps didn't get paid, in order to move forward.

Questions to Kick-Start Innovation

1. How would your culture react in this situation?
2. Is your compensation geared to independent innovation?

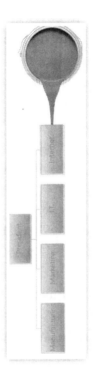

Turn the Org Chart on Its Side

"The achievement of excellence can occur only if the organization promotes a culture of creative dissatisfaction."
—Lawrence Miller

Earlier we discussed creating a separate organization if your new idea is big and disruptive. But what do you do when the idea grows up?

There are a number of choices.

SABRE chose to spin off Travelocity as a public company (and later decided it was too important to be separate and bought it back).

You can leave it separate and create a new division of the company.

REI had a wonderful idea. They created a separate Internet division, but when it grew up, the leader told me, "We turned the org chart on its side and poured the Internet in. We wanted everyone to be responsible for e-commerce and thus dissolved the Internet division." That might be the best result.

In the early 1900s, many companies had a department of electricity or a department of telephony. These new products were hard to manage and required oversight, but now they are gone. Taking your new idea back into the fabric of the company is like moving a new plant out of the greenhouse and into the garden, where it can grow big.

As the leader of a Fortune 50 entertainment company told me, "Why in the world in the twenty-first century do we still have an Internet department? We don't have a fax department! The Internet is a tool that everyone should be using."

This executive needs to turn his organization on its side!

Ronald Reagan famously said, "Mr. Gorbachev, tear down this wall." If you can't tear down the walls of your corporate divisions, you can create a new smaller organization focused on the future, as we did at Travelocity, and bring it back later.

Questions to Kick-Start Innovation

1. Would it be in your company's best interest to turn its org chart on the side? How could you innovate your organizational structure to be as current as possible?
2. Do you have something like an "Internet department"? A function that should be integrated into every department? What walls could be torn down in your business to make it operate better?

Ride the Bow Wave

*"Adventure must start with **running away** from home."*
—*William Bolitho*

Ever seen porpoises ride the bow wave of a ship? They are out in front using the pressure of the bow wave to push themselves along even faster than that huge tanker. They zip from one side to another, diving and turning much faster than the big boat, but without it they'd never reach that speed for so long.

At its best, innovation in a large corporation can be just like riding that wave.

You can use those parts of the company that can push you along much faster than you could ever go alone, and spin away from those things that might slow you down.

At Travelocity, even though we were small, we spent lots of time negotiating with huge airlines and hotel chains, so American's legal department was a big help. When we built our own building, American's facilities department did things we had no clue about. American's big name opened doors that would have been locked to a start-up. So riding the bow wave of the big company really helped in these areas.

Yet American's IT department was too expensive, their purchasing department too slow, and their advertising and PR departments really didn't "grok" the Internet customer. So in these cases we just spun away from the mother ship and did things on our own.

Leading innovation while working the corporate system requires some unique skills. Geoff Hunt, a senior VP of Sylvania, said about the head of his new ventures team, "I needed someone who was a bit of a dreamer, who could navigate our system."

So he hired Frank St. Onge to press their LED lighting business forward. LEDs will put Sylvania's replacement bulbs out of business…soon. According to *Fast Company* magazine, Frank broke a lot of eggs along the way, because he has his own packaging specialist and own logistics person. "I get somebody like the head of purchasing saying, 'Hey, your organization is the only one that has a purchasing person in it. That person needs to report to me.'" Onge ignores them.[23]

Providing air cover and working the corporate system is just part of the job when innovating in a large corporation.

Questions to Kick-Start Innovation

1. What corporate service can push your innovation forward, and where do you have to leave them behind?
2. How can you convince your boss to take the risk of going around the system?
3. Can you find innovators hiding in the departments you need to help you and get them to help you move quickly?

SECTION 7:

When All Is Said and Done, Make Sure More Is Done Than Said

"Genius is the ability to put into effect what is in your mind."
—F. Scott Fitzgerald

"Damnit, man, I expect my executives to be more open to new ideas than this."

Minimize Fear

"I'd be more brave if I wasn't so scared."
—Hawkeye in the TV show M*A*S*H

This final section is to address the obstacles that keep us from putting into effect the ideas in our mind and the innovations that would benefit our organization.

Fear of new ideas has been around as long as new ideas have. Which is why minimizing fear is part of the job description of any innovative leader.

In the early days of the Internet, just about all you read was how unsafe it was. We had a difficult time convincing SABRE's IT directors to allow us to connect SABRE to the Internet!

That may seem silly now, but their concerns were valid. After all, we were running some of the largest real-time systems in the world, and downtime or security issues simply weren't an option. For a time, it seemed no amount of "belt and suspenders" security filters would satisfy them. Over time, they came to agree that with great scrutiny, we could safely connect with the net.

We had a similar fear problem at Travelocity. When we started its predecessor, EAASY SABRE, we knew travel agents would be concerned about an online booking product. So our first iteration of the system allowed customers to make a reservation, but they had to send it to a travel agent to issue the ticket.

Since AOL and others were paying SABRE for providing the system, we even paid the agents a small incentive ($5) to service the booking (in addition to the commission that the airlines paid them for ticketing).

This worked for a while. But the agents really didn't grab on to the system. The bookings showed up in an obscure electronic file they never looked at. And as they didn't know these new customers and were busy on the phone with existing business, many times they just ignored the online reservations. Unfortunately, those online bookings expired and were cancelled, as they weren't ticketed. Customers were understandably upset.

When we started Travelocity and moved to the Internet, we knew the problem would be even bigger, so we created *our own* travel agency and gave the customer the choice of booking with us or with their local agent. The travel agent trade press thundered against us, but agents still were mostly unconcerned. Finally, in the interest of providing the best possible service, we eliminated the travel agency option and only issued tickets ourselves.

In retrospect, this "boil the frog slowly" process was an effective way to assuage the fear. If we'd started out eliminating the agents from the beginning, we would have had a big problem on our hands, and they would have fought us every step of the way.

Questions to Kick-Start Innovation

1. Do you have people on your project who fear the changes this innovation will bring? How are you addressing and assuaging those understandable fears?
2. Would a "boil the frog slowly" approach minimize fears?

Innovation Isn't Rocket Science

"This is rocket science."
—NASA

What NASA does is hard. It *is* rocket science. But innovation doesn't have to be difficult. I talk to many people who say, "I'm an engineer," or "I'm in finance." "I'm not the one who thinks up the ideas; I'm the one who makes them work."

They think innovation is a right-brained art, not a left-brained science. Actually, it's both. And *anyone* can do it.

Many times a big idea just involves changing part of an existing business model. Think about contact lenses. Were they rocket science? Price points changed, frequency of use changed, customer perception changed, but they're prescribed by the eye doctor, and you still buy them (mostly) from the same place you bought eyeglasses.

You buy cell phones from the same companies who sold you landlines. Travelocity is a registered travel agent. It sells differently than traditional agents, but in the end, that is what it is.

Kayak.com was founded after a discussion between the founders of Travelocity, Expedia, and Orbitz. We wondered what to do with all the visitors who searched us to find the right price and then went directly to the vendor (American, Hilton) to buy.

We thought, *There has to be a better way.* And there was. We simply built a site where customers could search everything they wanted and then buy directly from their supplier of choice. Kayak is (not unlike the examples above) a change to one part of the travel business model.

Rearden Commerce* added a rules engine to the travel booking process that positioned them as business travel specialists who report to corporations when employees violate their travel policy by travelling first class or staying at an exceedingly expensive luxury resort spa instead of a conference hotel. They expanded that process horizontally and also monitor dining, shipping, purchasing, limos, etc.

That was based on the simple idea that corporate purchasing departments who have for years controlled every penny of "hard good" costs needed the ability to control services costs as well.

Luxury Link* went beyond the normal selling of hotel rooms, to obtain rooms via barter advertising and then auction the rooms (after bundling additional services like transfers and spa treatments).

Smart Destinations* bundles tourist attractions so you can buy all the attractions in a city by the day and see everything at 40 percent off.

CheapOair (where I'm an advisor) is an online travel agency that actually pushes you to the telephone. Recognizing there are still a substantial number of travel customers who shop online and then would prefer to call, CheapOair built their own low-cost call center in India. They are nicely profitable mixing the web and the phone.

Priceline was just a travel agent, but it provided hotels and airlines with a way to get rid of unsold inventory without trashing the rest of their pricing.

Zipcar rents cars by the hour, and you can pick them up anywhere.

In each of these examples, someone took an existing business model and changed it slightly with dramatic results. These ideas were changes to pricing or customer service or the method of selling. So don't think that your job category gets you off the hook on innovating. Innovation can come from anywhere and be created in any department.

CAN YOU SIMPLY CHANGE THE BUSINESS PLAN?

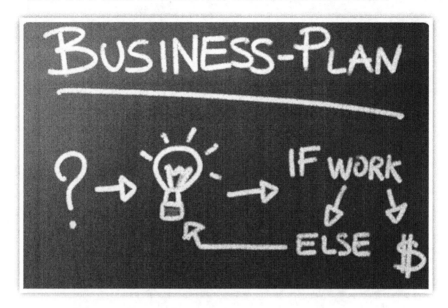

Questions to Kick-Start Innovation

1. Would you call yourself creative? Why or why not?
2. Do you have members on your team who think innovation is a right-brained activity and they're not good at it?
3. How will you educate your staff and coworkers that innovation is *not* rocket science? How will you imprint upon them that all you need is a brain and to keep your antenna up for a new way to do business?

* **I serve on the board of directors of each of these companies.**

IDEA 68

Sometimes You Are Just Too Early

"Who the hell wants to hear actors talk?!"
—*Harry Warner, Warner Bros. Pictures, 1927*

Innovation can be what Confucius called "searching for a black cat in a dark room." Sometimes the cat really isn't there, at least not yet.

Sometimes, as Harry Warner opined a few years before "talking pictures" changed movies forever, we're early in the game and can't imagine the game ever changing.

I've worked on several projects where we were sure our product was right on, but we were just too early. Sometimes the technology wasn't ready, and sometimes the customers weren't ready.

At the SABRE group, long before the Internet would make it a reality, we thought travelers would like to select cruises by watching videos, viewing graphic deck plans, and clicking to buy. So we built kiosks that did just that and put them in travel agencies. But the agents didn't want their customers getting used to self-service. They wanted to direct the sale and insisted we design desktop models. We did, but they were clunky and slow, and agents just didn't use them enough. We lost lots of money on that one. Of course, today the speed of the Internet makes self-service both possible and popular.

Another time, I thought customers of Travelocity would flock to a system that let them find the right day to travel and obtain the lowest fare. Rather than put in a specific date, they could just look at a calendar of the entire month and move their trip to the days with the low fares. I talked to many customers who told me it was a great idea. Since airline systems of that day could only answer airfare questions about a particular date, it took lots of time and money to create this product. And no one cared.

Perhaps it was simply too far beyond what people felt was possible. After all, customers were just getting used to booking online, and we rushed out another option. Perhaps they were overwhelmed, and we introduced an option too early in their learning curve.

We stayed the course for a while, given our investment. But neither promotion nor placement was a cure. Eventually we gave up. Yet today (almost fifteen years later), many travel sites have calendar shopping, and it is easy to see earlier and later in the week to see how much you can save.

I've now come to believe that visionary projects that don't make it the first time should be reviewed every six to twelve months to see if the world has caught up with them.

Perhaps the second or third time around, they will have evolved into an idea whose time has come.

Questions to Kick-Start Innovation

1. Have you ever pitched an idea that got turned down—and in retrospect, you realized the idea was just ahead of its time? What was the idea, and what happened?
2. Is it time to review and recycle that idea? Explain.

IDEA 69

You Can't Plan for Everything

*"It is impossible to live without failing at something, unless you
live so cautiously that you might as well not have lived
at all—in which case, you fail by default."*
—*J. K. Rowling*

No matter how well you've thought out your business plan, no
matter how much testing you've done, you will be surprised by
how much things can change in a way that you couldn't predict.

When it became clear that computer uptime was essential for
running a modern airline, American wanted the safest computer
center ever built.

So it was buried deep underground, there were backup gen-
erators, power from two separate grids, and banks of batteries.
To enter, you were required to both have a retina scan and be

weighed on a scale (to make sure you didn't steal anything). There was even a massive ice storage machine to continue to cool the computers if the chillers failed.

Disaster struck when a *raccoon* entered through a small duct, crawled deep into the center, and *ate* a critical control wire… crashing the entire system.

You can't plan for everything.

Travelocity launched with four buttons on the home page: Reservations, Destinations, Points of View, and Merchandise. We thought that was what people would want to accomplish: browse destinations, read critical reviews of potential locations, make a booking, and perhaps buy a suitcase or a travel item.

We could not have been more wrong. The *only* thing customers wanted to do was to make a reservation. Travelocity was at the time a joint venture with the company providing the destination information. We had to negotiate our way out of that deal, buy the URL from them, and completely change the layout of the site to reflect what the customer wanted. We kept to our core proposition but rejected all the rest, and quickly.

Over the first five years of our existence, our main source of income (travel agent commissions) was cut from 8 percent to 5 percent to *zero* by airlines looking to kill us. After each cut, we had to quickly remodel our business plan to not only replace that income but to continue to grow.

We could not have planned for these changes. Yes, instead of retreating and withdrawing to lick our wounds, we were flexible and nimble enough to pivot quickly and adapt accordingly. You can do the same.

Questions to Kick-Start Innovation

1. Have you had an idea or innovation fail? Did something you didn't plan for happen and undermine its success? How did that affect the team and company?
2. Did you reframe that failure as a lesson learned? How so? How did you pivot quickly and adapt to regain market share and revenue?

Victory of the Lilliputians

*"Leverage your brand. You shouldn't
let two guys in a garage eat your shorts."*
—Guy Kawasaki

Remember the Lilliputians? They were those little guys in the classic book *Gulliver's Travels* that successfully tied up the much larger Gulliver. They teamed up to have an advantage over his size, as there were so many of them and they moved fast.

American Express and Carlson Travel were the *only* national retail travel brands in the United States when Travelocity and Expedia came on the scene. They were the giants of travel.

Yet, in a few short years, our online brands were much better known, and within a decade we were both in the top ten travel agencies and closing in on AmEx. Today Expedia is the nation's *largest* travel agency, period.

How could this happen? Well, as in the book, AmEx (Gulliver) damn near lay down and let the Lilliputians tie him up.

Travelocity actually ran the AmEx online site for several years! I suppose AmEx didn't view the online world as either a threat or an opportunity. And yet they and Carlson ceded $50 *billion* in market share to Expedia, Travelocity, Priceline, and Orbitz.

One might say much the same is happening to Walmart. Look over this chart.

WAL★MART	amazon.com
#1 US Retailer ✓	#10 this year #19 last year ↑
Sales $408 Billion ✓	Sales $34 Billion
E Sales $8 Billion	E Sales $34 Billion ✓
200 MM Customers/Week ✓	137 MM Customers/week
#2 Retail brand	#1 Retail brand ✓
Growth FLAT	Growth 40% ✓

Walmart clearly leads in sales and is the number one US retailer. But Amazon is moving up fast and is the number one retail brand, with growth of 40 percent year over year. Most importantly, Amazon has four times the online sales of Walmart.

Walmart should be killing Amazon! They have ten times the purchasing power, the potential of a wonderful multichannel experience, and a footprint larger than anyone. They should have created a multichannel experience that wipes Amazon off the table. But they haven't, and I predict they won't. They've recently started another new online initiative, but the two executives, who'd been there a year, just quit.

Allstate Insurance is being proactive in order to try to remain free of the Lilliputians. Recognizing the problems of changing a large culture, they recently bought Esurance.

Follett (the textbook publisher) is reading the writing on the wall and bought an e-textbook company.

Will these catalysts be enough to keep them the giants in their industry? We'll find out, but at least they're taking pragmatic and visionary steps to remain successful and current. Are you?

Questions to Kick-Start Innovation

1. Is your company considered the giant in your industry? Who are the dominant organizations in your field?
2. What are you doing to maintain your size of the market share? Are you acquiring more current companies that could outgrow you or tie you up? How so?
3. What are you doing to be more nimble so you aren't lethargic and slow and vulnerable to visionary start-ups who could team together and pose a threat?

WALT DISNEY

Be a Dreamer and a Doer

"The world needs dreams and the world needs doers.
But what the world needs most is dreamers who do."
—*Sarah Ban Breathnach*

You've got to ship the product. Gordon Bennis called the development of the movie *Snow White* "a dream with a deadline."[24]

That's what innovation needs to be. You can't just have some vague idea of when you want to get your idea out in the world. At some point, the idea has to ship.

Sometimes it takes unwelcome-at-the-time external forces to motivate you to ship. We spent many years at AA developing the ability to price international airfares in SABRE. At the time international fares were so complex they could only be done by hand. The program was my responsibility, and I was frustrated by the endless stream of errors the program kept producing.

First, I discovered that since airfares changed every day, our testing was accomplished by testing new cases *every day!* We never tested the same thing twice. I fixed that. Even so, we still had a number of errors, too many to go to market. This went on for months. I was getting lots of pressure to ship. I finally looked at the problem another way. Having been an international tariff agent early in my career, I knew the complexity of fares made different agents produce different prices.

So instead of comparing the SABRE results against the price produced by *one* agent, I compared them against prices produced by *several* agents. Aha. Errors decreased. Then I compared them against the prices produced by an average agent vs. the best agent. Now they did very well. We shipped.

One of our ADS programmers was on deadline to write four custom reports. He just didn't see how he could do all of them in time. So he spent one thirty-six-hour stretch and wrote a report generator. Let the customers create their own reports, he thought! He made the deadline and created a killer product for us.

A friend told me, "That which can be done at any time rarely gets done at all." If you have no deadline, you have no sense of urgency. And most of us need a sense of urgency to move things to the top of our to-do list, which is the only way they'll get done.

Ship before you run out of time, money, or energy. Ship before your innovation becomes old hat or before circumstances change and render you obsolete before you start. Create your own external force if you need to, but put your idea on the line and ship. It is the only way your idea will become a reality and turn into an innovation that makes a dent in the universe.

Questions to Kick-Start Innovation

1. What is an idea or innovative project you're working on right now? Does it have a deadline to ship? What is that?
2. If it doesn't have a ship date, why not? Could you schedule milestones to chart progress so you have tangible proof the idea is moving forward? How so?

The Frisbee® Effect

*"Once you've done the mental work, there comes a point you have
to throw yourself into action and put your heart on the line."*
—Phil Jackson, *coach of the Los Angeles Lakers*

As we conclude this book, remember that *innovation is about putting ideas to work.*

As Phil points out, once you've done the mental work, you have to throw yourself into action and put your *idea* on the line.

We've all had that flash of inspiration where an idea popped into our head and we thought, "You know, someone should make that thing."

We've seen a problem or a need and thought, "*Somebody* should do something about that!"

Well, you're as much a somebody as anybody. Why don't *you* do something about that?

Growing up in the Chicago area in the '50s and '60s, our family fun was focused around Lake Michigan. Most every weekend in the summer, our family would head to the beach.

We'd leave first thing in the morning, bring the barbeque, and spend the day. A real treat in those days was to eat Jays potato chips along with our burgers and hot dogs.

To keep the chips fresh, Jays shipped them in a large, round can. And that can had a large, round lid.

One day, Dewitt and I took the lid and started tossing it back and forth like a discus. Amazingly, it flew really well. We started experimenting. After a few minutes we discovered how to hold it better and throw it for maximum lift and air time. Soon all the kids on the beach were playing with Jays lids.

My dad, brother, and I all saw how popular they'd become and said, "Gee we should turn this into a toy. We could make a lot of money."

We didn't. Wham-O Corporation did, and the Frisbee was born, one of the all-time most successful toys ever.

Why didn't we follow up on our idea?

Well, we were kids; we weren't inventors. My dad had a job; he was busy.

We kept playing with those lids summer after summer, talking about our idea and saying someday we were going to do something about it.

Then one day we saw the Frisbee at the store. We were crushed; someone had stolen our idea.

Nope, no one stole our idea. Someone was a doer! As the cartoon shows, the doer got up and left to get things done while the thinker's still sitting on his bottom, thinking about it.

Chuck Yeager, the first aviator to break the sound barrier, said, "At the moment of truth, there are either reasons or results." No more reasons why you *didn't* follow up on your idea. Just do it.

ACKNOWLEDGMENTS

Any book is a collaborative effort, so I have many people to thank.

First is my editor, Sam Horn. Sam, an accomplished author in her own right, found my voice and turned a manuscript into a book. For that I'm eternally grateful.

Many colleagues read and improved the manuscript, including my longtime mentor, business partner, and great friend, Kathy Misunas; my author and photographer brother, Dewitt; my agent, Monique Boucher; and, of course, my wonderful wife, Ginny, whose support was and always is very important.

Thanks to CreateSpace and BookBaby for crafting wonderful self-service products to allow me to produce a book just like I'd book a flight on Kayak.com...by myself!

I'd particularly like to thank Paul English and Steve Hafner, the founders of Kayak.com. Working with them over the past seven years has taught me so much about this fast-changing world of the web.

And finally, thanks to all the great people I've had the privilege to work with in all the companies I've been associated with over the years who have taught me so much about innovation.

ABOUT THE AUTHOR

Terry Jones is chairman of Kayak.com and founder of Travelocity. com. He's worked in the travel industry for forty years.

For the last ten years, he's been speaking and consulting with companies on innovation and change.

He had a twenty-year career at American Airlines and their SABRE division, serving in a variety of executive positions, including chief information officer.

A graduate of Denison University (in history), Terry started his career as a travel agent in Chicago after spending the year after college traveling around the world.

Shortly after entering the travel business, he cofounded a travel agency in Chicago specializing in travel to the Soviet Union. In five years it became a top business travel agency and a leader in automation.

He then jumped to information technology, accepting a job with a company that sold minicomputers to travel agents. When that company was sold to American Airlines, he began as a director in product marketing, later working as vice president of applications development and vice president of computer operations.

While at American and SABRE, he led the team of ten who began the development of Travelocity.com and, as CEO, took the company public.

Today he serves on five boards of directors, lectures, consults, and serves as an expert witness.

He lives with his wife, Ginny, near Lake Tahoe.

WANT TERRY TO SPEAK ON INNOVATION?

Terry is an accomplished speaker with twenty years of onstage experience. He's spoken to tens of thousands of people worldwide on the topics of innovation and building digital relationships with customers.

Some recent reviews:

"You brought so much passion and energy to our event in New York. I am certain our program in France will be all the more successful for your participation."
—*Ginni Rometty, CEO, IBM*

"His willingness to share his knowledge and his ability to open the minds of our audience and focus on their future...was remarkable."
—*ADP*

Watch Terry's videos and learn more about his programs and how you can have him speak at www.tbjones.com.

WE WANT TO HEAR FROM YOU!

Let's continue this conversation online at www.thebookoninnovation.com.

Did you break through the Bozone Layer? Hire some rock stars?

Begin to kill projects and not people?

Whatever you have to say about this book and about innovation, I'd like to hear it.

Stop by and let's talk.

Please take a moment to review this book on Amazon.com.
Good reviews help others find this book, so please tell others what you think of ON Innovation!

ENDNOTES

1. Adam Bryant, *The Corner Office*, St. Martin's Griffin
2. IBM Institute for Business Value
3. Hult & Malpuru, *Forrester US Online Retail Forecast 2009–2014*
4. www.supermarketguru.com
5. Life Insurance Marketing Association
6. IAB 2012 survey
7. IBM (IBM.com)
8. Wikipedia, "Think Different"
9. Rosabeth Moss Kanter, *Harvard Business Review*, July 2011
10. Leo Helzel, *A Goal Is a Dream with a Deadline*, McGraw-Hill
11. Bryant, *New York Times*, 3/13/2010 quoting Kip Tindell
12. *The Corner Office*
13. *The Corner Office*
14. Nagji and Tuff, *Harvard Business Review*, May 2012
15. Lefley and Charan, *The Game Changer*, Crown Business
16. *The Corner Office*
17. Salesforce.com website
18. Davenport and Manville, *Harvard Business Review*, April, 2012
19. The Bozone Layer comes originally from a Gary Larson *Far Side* cartoon. Its meaning has been enhanced over time.
20. Huston and Sakkab, "Connect and Develop," *Harvard Business Review*, March 2006

21. Babcock, *Information Week*, September 2011

22. Kidder, *Soul of a New Machine*, p. 280

23. Fitzgerald, *Fast Company*, April 2009

24. *Organizing Genius: The Secrets of Creative Collaboration*, with David Gergen

CPSIA information can be obtained at www.ICGtesting.com
Printed in the USA
LVOW07s1016190713

343709LV00008B/33/P